THE STORY OF MY REBIRTH

SUHAS'S

(ENGLISH AUTOBIOGRAPHY)

First Published in March 2022

ISBN: 978-93-5611-438-8

BLUEROSE PUBLISHERS

www.BlueRoseONE.com

info@bluerosepublishers.com

+91 8882 898 898

Cover Design:

Akash

Typographic Design:

Rohit

Distributed by: BlueRose, Amazon, Flipkart

LATE MR. GOPAL BALU JADHAV EX-SERVICEMAN SOLDIER INDIAN ARMY MY PATERNAL GRANDFATHER

LATE MR. VISHRAM HIRU (HIRAJI) PAWAR FORMER MILL WORKERMY MATERNAL GRANDFATHER

LATE MRS. RANJANA VISHRAM PAWAR MY MATERNAL GRANDMOTHER

Dedication

This Book Is Dedicated To My Mummy-pappa; My Grand Parents From Mummy-pappa Sides; My Whole Family; My Beloved Ones; Traditions; My Teachers; All My Friends And Supporters,

My Doctors; Almighty God; Nature; The Universe; All Energies; All Five Elements; All

Super
Powers And
Inspired By
The Physical; Mental; Economic Progress And Prosperity Of All Human Beings Of The World.....

....Suhas Surendra Sumita Jadhav

THE STORY OF MY REBIRTH

Special Thanks to

KEM HOSPITAL PAREL MUMBAI

NEUROSURGERY DEPARTMENT

Prof. Dr. Amit Mahore	MD / MS / Neurosurgeon / KEM Team / Parel / Mumbai

---

TATA HOSPITAL PAREL MUMBAI

RADIATION ONCOLOGY DEPARTMENT

Prof.: Dr. Rakesh Jalali	MD/MS/Oncologist/Radiation/ TATA /Parel / Mumbai
Prof.: Dr. Rajesh Uchil	MD/MS/Cardiologist Shivaji Park, Dadar (West)
Prof.: Dr. Ajay Dudhani	MD/MS/Eye Surgeon/Santacruz (W)
Dr. Veena Saraswat	MBBS / Mira Road / Thane
Prof.: Dr. Pramod Bhandari	MD/Skin/Dermatology/Mira Road / Thane
Prof.: Dr. Savita Goswami	Clinical Psychologist/Psycho Oncology / TATA / Parel/Mumbai
Prof.: Dr. Tejpal Gupta	MD/Radiation/Pathologist/TATA
Prof.: Dr. Hemant Telkar	MD/Radiologist/Jupiter/Dadar
Prof.: Dr. Manasi Takale	MD/Physiotherapy/TATA
Dr. Shashikant Chandanshive	MD / Physiotherapy / TATA
Smt. Nayana	Assistant / TATA
Prof.: Dr. Pravin Rangari	MS/General Surgeon

THE STORY OF MY REBIRTH

Prof.: Dr. Vijay Sarathi MD/Pathologist / KEM

Prof.: Dr. Amol MD/Nutritionist/KEM

THE STORY OF MY REBIRTH

Special Thanks To

Aai Grandmother Mrs. DEVKI GOPAL JADHAV

Prof.: Mrs. Samiksha Ravindra Suryavanshi / Sister

Prof. Ravindra Prakash Suryavanshi / Jiju

Mr. Dilip Vishram Pawar / Mama

Mr. Mahendra Laxman Jadhav / Mama

Mr. Dnyandev Vishram Pawar / Mama

Mrs. Navneeta Dnyandev Pawar / Mami

Mrs. Surekha Vishram Pawar / Mousi

Mr. Ravindra Gopal Jadhav / Chacha

Mr. Milind Gopal Jadhav / Chacha

Mr. Chandramani Gopal Jadhav / Chacha

Mr. Pramod Bhaguram Kamble / Mama

Mrs. Priyanka Pramod Kamble / Atya

THE STORY OF MY REBIRTH

Special Thanks To

ANUYOG SHIKSHAN SANSTHA

ANUYOG VIDYALAYA

Khar (East), Mumbai-400051.

Maharashtra/India

Principal /Prof.:Mr. Satishchandra Dattatray Chindarkar

Mrs. Rohini Satishchandra Chindarkar

Mr. Ashok Govind Khandekar / Panvel

Mr. Prakash Pandurang Nivate / Mira Road

Mr. Arvind Purushottam Sawant / Lower Parel

Mr. Anant Govind Kamble / Vasai

& Teaching - non Teaching Staff.

Mr. Pravin Shukla / Karate Coach / Mira Road

THE STORY OF MY REBIRTH

I am in Deep & Permanent Gratitude of....

1	Principal Mr. Satishchandra Dattatray Chindarkar
2	Mrs. Rohini Satishchandra Chindarkar
3	Principal Mr. Suryakant Laxman Joshi
4	Mrs. Shashi A. Sardesai
5	Principal Mr. Shivaji Shankar Rasal
6	Mr. Sudhir Yashwant Poyarekar
7	Principal Mr. Vasant Bhanudas Ingale
8	Principal Mr. Laxman Ganpat Pawar
9	Mrs. Usha Sahebrav Zele
10	Mr. Ashok Vasudev Khachane
11	Mr. Kisan Babu Satre
12	Principal Mr. Eknath Ramkrushna Kedar
13	Principal Mr. Arvind Purushottam Sawant
14	Principal Mr. Dilip Yashwant Jadhav
15	Mr. Dadasaheb Murlidhar Pawar
16	Mrs. A. A. Naik
17	Mr. Ashok Govind Khandekar
18	Mr. Anant Govind Kamble
19	Mr. Ganesh Nana Karvande
20	Mr. Bhanudas Kisan Patole
21	Mrs. Divya Deepak Sankhe
22	Mr. D. J. Banagar
23	Miss Meena Kamlakar Koli

24	Mr. Ramdas Sakharam Gethe
25	Mrs. Trupti Haresh Hambire
26	Mr. Madhukar Baburao Rupavate
27	Mrs. Smita Ramchandra Choramale
28	Mr. Gurunath Digambar Kudav
29	Mr. Dnyandev Anant Mungekar
30	Mr. Amod SH. Gosavi
31	Mr. Baban Dattu Sutar
32	Mr. Navnath Digambar Mungekar
33	Mr. Uma Rama Sarukte
34	Mr. Sunil Babaji Mayekar
35	Mr. Subhash Vishnu Pawar
36	Mr. M. G. Lingade
37	Mr. Pramod Ganpat Mahakal
38	Mrs. Anita G. Katkade
39	Mrs. Manisha S. Bahir – Ghevade
40	Mr. Vilas Tanaji Pawar
41	Mr. Harshal P. Devare
42	Mr. Mangesh SH. Dhamanaskar
43	Mr. Sunil B. Baviskar
44	Principal Mr. Ramchandra Adawale
45	Mr. Babaji Pawar
46	Prof. Dr.Prakash Salvi / Ruparel College
47	Prof. Dr.Varalu K.V. / L.S. Raheja College
48	Prof. Suresh Sawant / L.S. Raheja College
49	Prof. Dr. Rama Vishwesh / K.C. College

Dr. Rutuja Dalvi	Mrs. Vasudha Ghag
Mrs. Amrin Kakalmeli	Mrs. Renuka Harmalkar
Mrs. Ashwini Salian	Mrs. Enid Madam
Mr. Pravin Shukla	Mr. Y. M. Koman
Dr. Prashant Ghorpade	Mrs. Greta Pharel
Mr. Nikhil Kamble (Chef)	Mrs. Luiza Tuscano
Mr. Prathamesh Gharat	Mrs. Loreta Pinto
Mr. Shiraj Manjrekar	Mrs. Sibil Furtado
Mr. Rupesh Bhosle	Mrs. Trupti Patil
Mr. Durgadas Rathod	Mr. Abhishek More
Ms. Sneha Kudtarkar	Mr. Mangesh Choudhari
Ms. Santoshi Kadam	Mr. Vinay Dwivedi
Mr. Pranit Dhopte	Mrs. Ruhee Shaikh
Mr. Umesh Tirmali	Mr. Ramchandra K. Bhosle
Dr. Ashish Mishra	Mrs. Seeta R. Bhosle
Mr. Akash Ambre	Mr. Prakash R. Bhosle
Mr. Nandkumar D. Sankhe	Mrs. Suman Arun Kurle
Mr. Vilas G.Rahate	Mrs. Asha Sanjay Pawar

Prof. Mr. Ganesh Tukaram Patil
Prof. Mr. Sakharam P. Patil
Prof. Mrs. Pranali P. Parab/Joshi
Prof. Mr. Santosh M. Parab
Prof. Mr. Bhanudas N. Pawar
Prof. Mrs. Amruta Ganu
Mr. Prakash Pandurang Nivate
Mrs. Neelam M. Chindarkar/Narvekar
Mrs. Vidya S. Parab / Jadhav
Mrs. Priyanka P. Rajam/Malankar
Mrs. A. J. Wadekar / Panchal
Mrs. Vaibhavi V. Gawade / Raut
Mr. Mahesh M. Mulmule
Mrs. Kavita SH. Ingale
Mrs. Vishakha SU. Jadhav
Mrs. Kumudini Ramnath Parkar
Mr. Deepak Patil & Mr.Dashrath Borade
Anuyog Shikshan Sanstha Khar (E) Mumbai.
Anuyog Marathi High School – Staff
Anuyog English High School – Staff
Anuyog Employees Credit Co. Society Ltd.
Secondary Employees Credit Co. Society Ltd.

My Dear & Respected Doctors who tried their best to save my life and kept me safe

Prof. Dr. Amit Mahore Sir Md/Ms/Neurosurgeon
Kem Hospital Parel Mumbai

My Dear & Respected Doctors who tried their best to save my life and kept me safe

PROF. DR. RAKESH JALALI
SIR MD/MS/RADIATION
ONCOLOGISTTATA
MEMORIAL HOSPITAL
PAREL MUMBAI

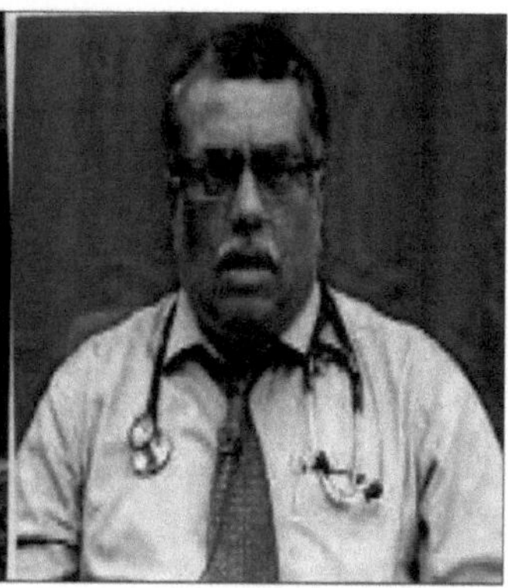

PROF. DR. RAJESH
UCHIL SIR
MD/MS/CARDIAOLOGIST
SHIVAJI PARK
DADAR MUMBAI

PROF. DR. HEMANT TELKAR
SIRMD/ RADIOLOGIST
JUPITER DADAR MUMBAI

PROF. DR. TEJPAL GUPTA
SIR MD/RADIATION
ONCOLOGIST /
PATHALOGISTTATA
MEMORIAL HOSPITAL
PAREL MUMBAI

My Dear & Respected Doctors who tried their best to save my life and kept me safe

PROF. DR. AJAY DUDHANI SIR MD/MS/EYE SURGEON SANTACRUZ WEST MUMBAI

PROF. DR. SAVITA GOSWAMI MADAMCLINICAL PSYCHOLOGIST TATA MEMORIAL HOSPITALPAREL MUMBAI

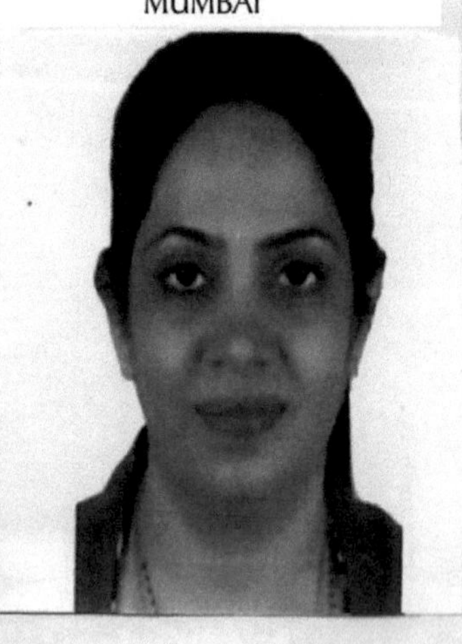

PROF. DR. PRAMOD BHANDARI SIRMD/SKIN / DERMATOLOGIST MIRA ROAD, THANE

DR. VEENA SARASWAT MADAMMBBS GENERAL PHYSICIAN OUR FAMILY DOCTOR MIRA ROAD THANE

My Dear & Respected Doctors who tried their best to save my life and kept me safe

ADVOCATE MR. PRAVIN SHUKLA SIRMY KARATE COACH GUIDE AND MOTIVATER

I AM WITH MY DEAR AND RESPECTEDSURGEON DR. AMIT MAHORE SIRAFTER MY RECOVERY

I AM WITH MY DEAR AND RESPECTEDDR. RAKESH JALALI SIR IN TAJ HOTEL AFTER MY RECOVERY

I AM WITH MY PHYSIOTHEROPIST DR. MANASI TAKALE MADAM, NAINA MADAM & JAYASHRI MADAM

Our Dear & Respected Personalities Who Tried Their Best To Support Us

OUR GOD FATHER FOUNDER OF ANUYOG SHIKSHAN SANSTHA DIRECTOR WINNER OF PRESIDENT'S AWARD FOR BEST TEACHER EDUCATIONIST MOTIVATER PRINCIPAL MR. SATISHCHANDRADATTATRAY CHINDARKAR SIR

OUR GOD MOTHER CO-FOUNDER OFANUYOG SHIKSHAN SANSTHA DIRECTOR EDUCATIONIST MOTIVATER HEAD MISTRESS MRS. ROHINISATISHCHANDRA CHINDARKAR MADAM

OUR DEAREST FRIEND FINANCIAL MENTAL SUPPORTER TEACHER MR. ASHOK GOVIND KHANDEKAR SIR

OUR DEAREST FRIENDTEACHER SUPPORTER MR. PRAKASH PANDURANG NIWATE SIR

OUR DEAREST FRIEND
TEACHER SUPPORTER PRINCIPAL
MR. ARVIND PURUSHOTTAM
SAWANT SIR

OUR DEAREST FRIEND TEACHER
SUPPORTER MR. ANANT
GOVIND KAMBLE SIR

My Dear Relatives And Loved Ones Who Tried Their Best To Save My Life And Kept Me Safe

MY PATERNAL GRAND MOTHERAAI DEVAKI GOPAL JADHAV

MY PAPPA / FATHER MR. SURENDRA GOPAL JADHAV

MY MUMMY / MOTHERMRS. SUMITA SURENDRA JADHAV

MY DIDI / SISTERPROF. SAMIKSHA RAVINDRA SURYAVANSHI

MY JIJU / BROTHER-IN- LAW
PROF. RAVINDRA PRAKASH
SURYAVANSHI

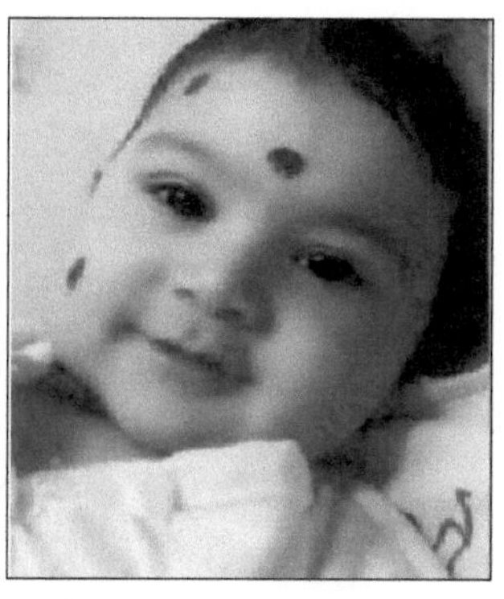

MY NEPHEW / SISTER'S SON
BALA / LADKU MASTER
AHARTARAVINDRA
SAMIKSHA SURYAVANSHI

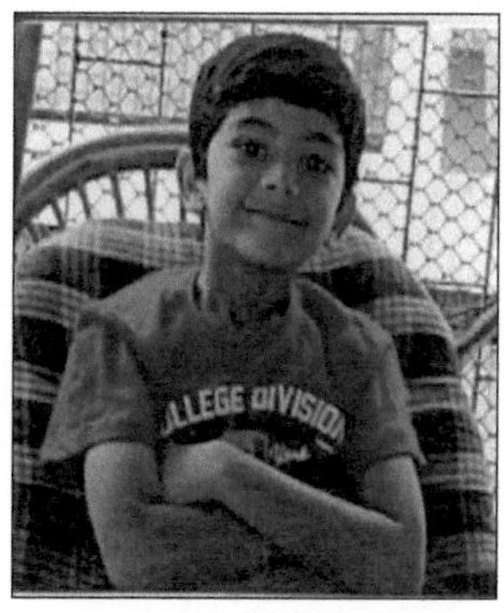

MY NEPHEW / SISTER'S SON
BALA / LADKU / MASTER
AHARTA RAVINDRA
SAMIKSHA SURYAVANSHI

My Dear Relatives And Loved Ones Who Tried Their Best To Save My Life And Kept Me Safe

MY PATERNAL UNCLE - 1 MR. RAVINDRA GOPAL JADHAV

MY PATERNAL UNCLE - 2 MR. MILIND GOPAL JADHAV

MY PATERNAL UNCLE - 3 MR. CHANDRAMANI GOPAL JADHAV

MY PATERNAL ANTY - 4 MAI/BABY/ATYA MRS. PRIYANKA PRAMOD KAMBLE

MY PATERNAL UNCLE-IN-LAWMAI ATYA'S HUSBAND MR. PRAMOD BHAGURAM KAMBLE

My Dear Relatives And Loved Ones Who Tried Their Best To Save My Life And Kept Me Safe

MY MATERNAL UNCLE -1 MR. DNYANDEV VISHRAM PAWAR - MTNL

MY MATERNAL AUNTY -1 IN-LAW MRS. NAVNEETA DNYANDEV PAWAR

MY MATERNAL UNCLE -2 MR. MAHENDRA LAXUMAN JADHAV - BPT

MY MATERNAL UNCLE -3MR. DILIP VISHRAM PAWAR - BEST

MY MATERNAL AUNTY- 4 (MOUSHI)MRS. SUREKHA VISHRAM PAWAR - TAILOR

THE STORY OF MY REBIRTH.....

I, Suhas Surendra Sumita Jadhav,

I still remember that day singing Competition was there in Vartak College, Vasai. I decided to take part in the competition. My friend 'Ashish Satpute' himself was one of the co-ordinator. He was looking after the whole competition. I told him to call my name for performance after two three students perform their songs and he did accordingly. My name was called and my friends clapped. Judges were surprised. I came, I sang the song. I told them and I left for home. Today was my appointment with Dr. Rajesh Uchil, Cardiologist, at Dadar Shivaji Park. I came home and said mummy that my song I sung was like OK; fine. But I was unaware about the C.T. Scan. Pappa had taken my C.T. Scan and report on 16th July 08 itself. But I wasn't ready to come to Dr. Rajesh Uchil at Dadar. Mummy kept a condition, if I am coming for the appointment then and then only they (mummy papa both) will come for their appointment. Both mummy papa had their checkup at Dr. Rajesh Uchil's Namita Clinic. In the evening we went to Dadar by local train. I was facing trouble, pain while climbing the floor steps of the railway station and bridge. Dilip mama, mummy, pappa and me came to Namita Clinic by taxi.

I was a Karate 1st Dan Black Belt and referee license holder. Last twelve years my elder sister Samiksha didi and myself were taking Marshal Art training in Shotokan Karate Association of India (SKAI). I was head boy in 2004-05 year of my school Cardinal Gracias High School, Bandra East, Mumbai. So I was known to every teacher and each and every student of our school. I took part in all cultural activities, programs, sports, singing etc. and was in everybody's eyes. I was favorite student of all the teachers. My sister Samiksha was House Captain (Purple) of our school in 2002-03 year. So "her brother is Suhas" made me double famous. My school Cardinal Gracias High School is in Bandra. We were also from there. But after the death of my grand-father we were staying in slum for two three years. Also Pappa took 2-BHK house on loan at Mira Road in 2003-04. As toilet was common there we were facing problem in the slum and were uncomfortable. Also Samiksha didi had her 12th H.S.C. year and myself 10th S.S.C. year. So we decide to shift from 09-06-2004 and we started living at Mira Road Thane. New people, new surroundings, new house and new problems, too! But we were knowing how to face problem and we risk we gain! Those days were different. Getting up at 4:30 a.m. in the early morning, getting ready, running for autorickshaw, then crowdy local train! It was really a difficult situation. Travelling by train was so difficult that because of crowd, it was tough to get stand on the gate of the compartment (boggie) itself. But we had hope and what we accepted we had to follow. Pappa started using Season Ticket (3 monthly Pass) of First Class. I was able to travel in first class bogie with second class pass accordingly to the rule, as I was in uniform of my school. Now we were at least able to get inside the local train. Now days went and the year was complete we were unknown that when the year passed away. Then on 26th July 2005, I was unable to get admission of Diploma Engineering in Bandra Polytechnic. In that heavy rain pappa and me went to Bandra East house in the slum. My Grandmother, my Uncle Milind bhaee and his family, my another uncle Ravindra anna's children and my (aunty's) Mai attya's family were staying there. In that heavy rainfall whole Mumbai city was over flowed, flooded and was water logged. Chest level water was collected in the slum where we were halting (4 feet). It was increasing water level. It was dark outside. All the doors of the houses were closed. With the discussion with Pappa and his permission I decided to get into the water. We had taken dinner early. Pappa told everyone to have as much as everyone could because it was emergency time and when we will get food to eat next we didn't know. We were sleeping and water started coming from the ground. Pappa was sleeping down touching feet to the door. He thought that of water comes in the house; it will enter from the door. But it came up from the ground first instead of the door. Now we opened the door and saw outside. It was dark and water everywhere. I had told pappa before and I did what I said. I got into the water which was around my neck. It was continuously raining. I reached more than 5 to 6 (1 + 1 floor) slum row houses in neighbour and asked them if they had empty space for us to stay for one night. But everyone said no to me. Pendulkar aunty's house was at the end of the lane. She was knowing us and was pre-primary teacher also. She told only ladies and children can occupy space that much space is only available. I straight came to tell pappa and all in water. Now it was the real test. All dirty logged water which was more than 5 feet, and in that it was raining continually and also dark night. I told everyone that I will carry each of five, children on my shoulder to Pendulkar aunty's house and I did it. It was the level of water where the children's height was insufficient and they were drowning. Then pappa, uncle Milind bhaee and me carried my grandmother keeping her dry as much as could and reached Pendulkar aunty's house. Behind then my aunty Geeta Kaki carrying her daughter, pappa's sister Mai Attya and Nisha (tai) came. Now this house which was on the first floor got crowded and was housefull. So pappa and uncle Milind bhaee sat on the iron ladder and I was sitting in the edge of the floor near the door. That night each second was like an hour for me and everybody. We were pissed off that night. But I had saved lives of five and pappa stood as a wall to protect the family in this life threatening situation. The next day slowly the sun was rising. Night was leaving and darkness was expelling. So also water level was decreasing. And at last decreased at around 10 a.m. in the morning Pramod mama (Aunty's) Attya's husband came home. He was fully wet and was stuck-up in flood at Andheri in a BEST bus. Vasai's Uncle Chandramani Appa my Pappa's younger brother came to see us at Bandra. His wife was in the flood on the Western Express Highway and was walking with lakhs of Mumbaikar who suffered the flood situation. But a gentleman gave her place in his car who felt pity about her and took her to his house and she was saved. Dilip mama also came to see us from Mahim. Everybody was saved. In this way, every single life was saved by pappa and me and we returned to Mira Road home. As soon as we came home mummy hugged pappa tightly. It was true that mummy had faced a greatest challenge that night.

In all that situation, I lost my Diploma Engineering admission and I had cancelled my admission before only of Vartak College Vasai. Then I placed admission in the Mahatma Phule's Technical Schools Junior College at Parel. Again my travelling had started. I felt tired each and every day. I went to tution classes every evening. I was conducting Karate Class also. My time table was disturbed. No food on time. Hectic long travelling daily. No rest, no ample and complete sleep. And my body's immunity level started decreasing. I suffered "jaundice disease" in my childhood. For that I was admitted to the hospital also. Again now I suffered with Jaundice. Pursuing it Typhoid fever caught me in its web and I was broken down. We were not able to understand. Bearing all in this situation I went of Karate Class those days. I had also suffered from chickenpox. HSC 12th std. year was hectic for me and was having minimum rest time and for engineering admission pappa and I went till Aurangabad but were unsuccessful. I had cleared HSC 12th board exam. But engineering admission had become a dream to me again. Now I started B.Sc. studies at Vartak College, Vasai. But till then I was broken down physically and mentally both the ways. I had lost endaevour. My immune system collapsed and immunity level started to answer. My hair started getting white which was not big deal in small age where one or two white hair were present. But now bunch of hair started to get white. And first time my eyesight was affected and the few seconds of blackout started coming. I couldn't see anything in those few seconds of blackout. I started falling weak and falling down having no strength in for minutes. We first thought because of weakness these things are happening. Pappa, mummy were having many thoughts in their minds and were restless for me. I was having abnormal behavior and started unnatural habits during like moving neck to one side every time. Getting dizziness frequently, imbalance in daily normal activities like walking, standing straight etc. Frequent acidity, pain in spine and back. I had taken light at Jain Health Centre Dadar for my back hip pain recently. My normal behavior was also drastically changed and I started getting angry. I started getting irritated and tempered. I had lost interest in life, day to day living because the day to day things which everyone was doing easily, I couldn't do so. I kept quiet and motionless, activity less. I slept on the bed for hours just thinking what's going on. On the whole my physical activities were stopped and started being lonely. Continuous headache and forehead having fever made me several times go to B.H.M.S. Mrs. Dr. Goyal nearby and she gave me fever and headache tablets. I took it for many weeks and days but had no improvements. Many times she said after typhoid fever, head is found to be warm occasionally. I had complaints regarding piles too. We had a checkup and B.A.M.S. Dr. Rajesh Raut nearby denied those issues that I have piles. Then why was I so weak going? This question was troubling all of us.

Once Mayur my cousin (Bhayandar's Mahendra Mama's son) had come at our place. We were talking in the middle room and I just went to the mirror. That time I felt my lips are shivering; moving. This was not at all normal. My eyes were squinting I felt. My right hand's thumb had no sensation at all. I was pinching; pressing but I had no feeling. My lips again became normal and I came out and told my mummy about this when we applied Amritanjan balm to the thumb. I just took the vigorous smell a bit and in seconds it was blackout. My eyes were open but I wasn't able to see anything. We all got scared and afraid.

BAMS Dr. Rajesh Raut nearby was brought home. He checked me and gave tabs and injection. On 1st Jan. 2008 we went to Dr. Reshma Patil at Silver park. She is a MBBS doctor. She gave a protein supplement named "Protein X' which was also given by Dr. Mrs. Goyal (BHMS). Due to continuous headache now I started Dr. Reshma Patil's (Silver Park Mira Road) treatment and taking tablets given by her. Manna Powder which is mixed in milk and taken was also given to me by her. After taking course of medicine, there was no effect on my headache and we again went to her. That time she commented about me that, "Suhas still going on is because of this Protein supplement". Hearing her words mummy was surprised and started thinking why must have she said like this about me?" Her words touched my mummy. After thinking and discussion we decided to visit Dr. Rajesh Uchil MD/Cardiologist Namita Clinic, Dadar. He met me, saw me, checked me and gave tablets for headache. But it was unstoppable and in a month itself we again went to Dr. Rajesh Uchil and immediately he told to do a C.T. Scan of my brain. On 14th July 2008, my brain's C.T. Scan was done at Jupiter Center Dadar. Still I was attending my Vartak College at Vasai and was traveling daily. I was not able to stand for more than 2 hrs for practical. Physics, Chemistry and Mathematics were my subjects.

In the year from 2007 to 2008, I was habitual of moving my neck in a particular direction frequently. In case of neck pain I am moving my neck frequently was abnormal and on 15th August 2007 my cousin Bharat's birthday, his aunty Asha marked that my neck moving habit was abnormal. There we came to know that Aaee (my paternal grandmother) also had told pappa to take me to the doctor for my neck. That time itself, I was suffering from severe back pain, hip pain and by the guidance of Orthopedic Dr. Apurva Desai – Shree Nursing Home Dadar, I took light at Jain Health Centre Dadar for 10 days. My 12th Std (HSC). year (2006-07), went in health complaints taking treatments and hectic travelling. Dr. Kinjal Shah Jain Health Center Dadar guided her assistant for the light treatment. In that year, I was restless, hunger decreased; thought it's because of Jaundice and so my Liv52 tablet was also on. Because of headache I had checked my eyes at eye Surgeon and had taken number spectacle and started using it. After all these efforts and treatments also, my headache was not stopped. And my health was affected more and more. Then also I was travelling, reading, walking and doing my daily routine works on my strength. Afterwards a X-ray was also taken of my head. It showed nothing. Dr. Mrs. Goyal was guiding us accordingly , we did, but I was unable to understand that exactly what was happening to me and my body? I felt sleepy every time. My interest was lost in normal activities also. There was no wish; no desire left in my life now. Then also due to my mummy, pappa, Samiksha didi and family's talking; I tried doing work and helping mummy in house hold works as possible. My Karate Class was at Bandra Cardinal Gracious High School and my Junior College was at

Bhoiwada Parel Mumbai. So much stress; so much travelling; hard work and still I managed to score 65% marks in 12th HSC board examinations in Science faculty. It was Mahatma Phule Junior College Bhoiwada Parel. Due to all above routine my lunch, dinner and breakfast was not on time or rather was skipped. Because of zero rest my body, endevour and health was affected. I was reduced. My body was reduced and I started looking abnormal and thin. One day my mami (Dakshata/ (Dilip Mama's wife) came home when she was surprised and told mummy that "Bhaoo (myself) is looking so ill, thin and sick." There was no effect of any doctor's treatment on me. Everybody was worried. There was birthday celebration of Dilip mama's children at his place nearby. They were playing songs with full volume. It was OK for all but not for me. I felt it unbearable. My head was paining and was restless. Everyone knew I am not comfortable and so I came home. I remain restless. Talking, laughing and walking with anyone had completely stopped. I was unable to get admission in Engineering so was sad and now it was impossible and difficult for me to come out of this depression. Not a single friend was there with me with whom I can share my feelings and make my mind free. This made me mum and dumb more. I sat on place hours and kept quite. I would speak few words with my didi (sister Samiksha) and my mummy and pappa. So everyone came under tension. So they three decided to celebrate my birthday outside on 6th May 2008. A change for me they thought and planned to spend whole day out. On that day I took a new pair of shoes worth Rs. 700/- at Mira Road Railway Station.

We four went to Borivali Sanjay Gandhi National Park. We did boating in the river lake. Pappa and me sat in one boat and mummy; didi sat in another. We had to give padd ling like bicycle to the boat to keep it moving. Same time, same place a couple was boating and their boat went into the mud and got stuck. Both of them got out side and were pushing their boat. I smiled watching them little bit. Mummy and didi laughed but my laughing also became painful and difficult for me now because it brought pressure on my head and whole body. So I started keeping quiet and silent. After boating we went to Tiger Safari. While moving in jungle in a Van we saw tigers, cheetahs, white tigers, lions and many other animals. I was just trying to enjoy but I was not at all fine that time and was bearing pain in my head and whole body. Headache was continuous. Then also I was showing that I am happy. There were many deers in one of the cages. We gave carrots to them and we also were feeding those sensitive dears. They were really cute. Beside there was another cage where in a female cheetah was kept. Her stomach was big and she was slowly roaring also. Everyone who came to see thought she is sick but after returning back home I told mummy, pappa and didi that she is pregnant. Fact that after two months she gave birth to two cubs of cheetahs and this news was given on Doordarshan T.V. That day on my birthday we took lunch in the hotel. We sat in the mini train 'Van Rani' and took snaps of each other. Didi, Mummy, and Pappa shouldn't get sad or upset so I was pretending to be fine and happy. Afterwards we sat in the garden of the National Park. Then pappa asked me whether I wish to see movie in theatre or go anywhere else? I said no and we came home. My mind and heart was slide down to the great extent. Many negative thoughts were coming in my mind. I felt to rest on the bed for hours in that position. I had lost myself from me. I was finding and searching what has happened to me. I was trying to find the reason. Also our financial condition was not good at that time. Staying in a new house and after four years also I was willing to go to Bandra always. Same time our building renovation and sliding window work was going on. It was not done properly and we were unsatisfied. We had lost money and had loss in it. Financial problems increased more. Pappa was trying to cope up with the situation very hard. We all were low. Because of my health problem, I was tensed more. Mummy, pappa, didi and all were tensed. Pappa's school, Samiksha didi's studies, travelling hecticness, less sleep made vanish the actual homes of our house. Due to regular problems we were under tension. In such condition pappa went to Dadar to bring my C.T. Scan and report. But when he came to know about the actual problem what happened there? When he describes "thrones poke us none". On 16th July 2008 pappa went to Dr. Hemant Telkar. He said Suhas has a Tumour in the brain. When he heard tumour in the brain', his legs started to shiver. He was shocked for a minute. He became sad. The sky of sorrow fell on him. Aaee (Grandmother), mummy, myself and didi (sister) were unaware of this. Dr. Hemant Telkar gave water to drink pappa and told him to sit on chair and made him calm first and suggested to remove the tumour. And he said 95%of this is no life threat but 5% he can't tell anything. Thereafter listening these words, pappa again had hopes. He immediately took decision and decided to act according to the guidance of Dr. Rajesh Uchil and Dr. Hemant Telkar. But what he will say pappa was unaware of that. We took appointment of Dr. Rajesh Uchil. In the evening we reached his clinic. I was observing other patients. They were normal ones. I was thinking why I am not like them? And also thought when the day will come when I will be normal and my health better. I still remember that moment very clearly. We went to the Dr. Rajesh Uchil's cabin after our number came. Dr. Rajesh Uchil saw the scan and report and smiled to me, and said that there is a problem. I fearlessly asked him what issue? He replied that my brain in swollen there is a tumour in my btain. You have to do an urgent surgery of it. I again asked him "Can't it get fine through radiation (light) or tablets? He replied that surgery is necessary. It's Ok fine! I answered him normally and very lightly. Then mummy questioned Dr. Rajesh Uchil. He replied that there is one patient in a thousand who has this problem. Dr. Rajesh Uchil told me to sit outside. What exactly they were talking inside, I didn't know. Dr. Rajesh Uchil told pappa, mummy and Dilip mama that operation is must. Either it's done in private hospital or done in government hospital, the operation will be same. If operation is done in private hospital then the charges are more and not affordable for middle class people who are common. So he gave a reference note for K.E.M. hospital's Neurosurgery department head Dr.Atul Goyal, Senior Doctor's Dr. Dattatray Mujumdar and Dr. Trimurty Nadkarni. Dr. Rajesh Uchil is a MD Cardiologist and had practiced 15 years in K.E.M. hospital, Parel, Mumbai. He was knowing all the heads and seniors doctors of K.E.M. Taking the note we came out. It was night and so we went to a hotel and sat for a while. There pappa ordered Idli Sambar. We were all tensed. We took time. We had no desire of having snacks. Pappa told mummy to have snacks but she was under tension hearing words of Dr. Rajesh Uchil till now. She was not feeling well and had "nausea"(vomit feeling). But she didn't tell us that time and didn't eat anything. Because of unbearable travelling for me, we discussed and decided that me and mummy would stay at Mahim that night. Leaving us at Mahim, Dnyandev mama's house pappa and Dilip mama went to Mira Road by local train. Pappa told Samiksha didi that he is coming and won't have dinner. That night Dilip mama told didi to prepare Sandwich for pappa. That night of mine went in thinking and tensed one. Mummy too wished not to have food because she was also not willing to have it. Then mummy called my maushi Surekha at her tailoring shop Bandra. And she also came soon. Whole night everyone was tensed. Each and every moment was like an hour for us. We didn't know about next morning what was going to happen!

Both mummy pappa decided to take me out of this situation. Pappa also spoke with Dilip mama that we must do the action immediately and do the operation surgery. For this we must get ready. Morning of 17/7/2008 was an important incident of my life. Early morning I got up that day and to go K..E.M. Hospital we began to get ready. At Mahim, toilet facility was common and outside. So my maushi Surekha and my mami Navneeta were with me. After finishing my routine work, I got up and suddenly blackout came on my eyes. I shouted and called "Maushi!" I can't see anything!" Hearing this both Maushi Surekha and my mami Navneeta got scared and were afraid off. They both brought me back home catching my hands and till then I became normal again. When they told mummy about the incident, she said them that "like this, is happening daily". This problem won't go, won't end and won't finish without operation. Early morning pappa and Dilip mama reached Mahim home. At 7'O clock in the morning we reached K.E.M. Hospital Parel, Mumbai. My paternal uncles (pappa's younger brothers) were already reached there. My Atya's (Pappa's sister) husband (Pramod mama) was also with them. My all three mamas (maternal uncles) (Mummy's brothers) and my maushi (Mummy's sister) all came running that morning for me. To bring case paper two of them went. My case file was given in the O.P.D. department. As it was early morning, I was first patient and I was called inside. Dr. Abida Shah and Dr. Paresh were the doctors. They told me to sit. They started their checking and for one hour they examined me. They hit my knee and elbow with a hard rubber attached hammer to the steel rod. They asked me my past history and present. And then they told other doctors something word "glioma" in their medical language. I heard it clearly. But that time I was unaware of its meaning. Immediately after O.P.D. checkup they told us to do my M.R.I. of brain. And so I was again in tension. They told its an emergency MRI, so everyone was tensed and started to run for help. Mahendra mama went to M.R.I. department and told them about the emergency; why urgent MRI is necessary and took appointment. One and half hours my MRI took to finish. This was my first M.R.I. I fearlessly faced this whole thing. I thought my operation will be a small and simple one. It will get complete and soon and I will be back to my college. I was unknown of the seriousness and complications and what exactly has happened to me. I was told to sleep on the M.R.I. machine bed. It goes inside the machine. The machine was big circular shape and was magnetic. In that room my pappa was only present. No metal thing was allowed with him they told. There was another room attached to this. In that the M.R.I. machine technicians and doctors were sitting in front of the computers. Both rooms were joined by a glass partition and they could see me. They spoke and gave instructions through intercom; mike. Sound of M.R.I. machine is much louder and one can become deaf for a while. So, I was given cotton balls to keep in my ears. When I laid, my both ears were covered with tight sponge and an IV was injected and attached to my hand to give injection (IV is a way made to give injection without a needle). First half of M.R.I. was done for plane brain films. The sound of the machine is like same as the background sound given to the Hindi Bollywood movie "Ghajni" when names are shown in beginning. I was shivering as the room was fully air-conditioned. Then through IV a contrast injection was given to me. So that the scan images would come more clear. My M.R.I. took 1 ½ hours to complete. As they told, afterwards I was taken for blood test centre beside the hospital. It was lunch time so everyone (total 11 people) sat at Aditi Hotel for lunch opposite K.E.M. Hospital. We ordered less spicy vegetable and roti. After taking my blood reports and M.R.I. brain reports again we went to doctors of K.E.M. Hospital. Doctor told me to get admit to the ward immediately and gave a reference note " Admit immediately". With that note we came to the K.E.M. hospital's 2nd floor, 10 No. Ward. Nurses of blue, red and green belts were present. Reading the note they admitted me. Till then it was evening. Now we told my uncles and mamas to go back home. Pappa, mummy and maushi were with me now. My Ward No. was 10 as well as my bed no. was 10. It was a special ward of brain and spine patients. Continuously operations were going on and they were taking patients to the O.T. (operation theatre) and bringing back. Such scene made us afraid a little bit. Whole night I wasn't able to sleep. There were doctors meetings going on, discussion going on regarding my operation. The night was scary one. 18th July, 2008 Friday, the sun rised. My head was paining, I was restless, It was continuously paining, unstoppable. I was given injections and medicines via saline. As everyone came to know about me, relatives came running to see and meet me in K.E.M. hospital. Pappa's school colleagues teachers staff also came to see me. Seeing this ward doctors and nurses started shouting and got angry. They immediately ordered everyone to empty the ward and go out. On that day this situation happened around 10 to 11 times. Doctors were irritated and told to take me home because other patients in the ward were disturbed and were facing inconvenience. "Tell everyone to come home and see him". Mummy Pappa then apologized the doctors. Now whoever was coming to see me, they both strictly send one person in the ward at a time and only to see me from far and let go out quietly without speaking. I was told to fast 12 hours before operation. The whole day I was hungry and was waiting for my turn for operation. But because of their timetable and emergency cases, my operation was postponed. After whole day fasting and being hungry, I was told to eat and drink water at around 12'O clock in the night. At nearby hotel pappa went and brought Chinese Veg. fried rice. I ate it as possible as I could and drank lots of water. That night I had a nice sleep. At the Sunrise on 19th July 2008, Saturday, there first time I met my surgeon Dr. Amit Mahore sir. He came to see me and meet me. He told me and pappa that he was going to do the operation surgery. And with smiling face he left the ward. Everything which is done before operation was done to me. A list was given by the staff to pappa. It was list of medicines, saline bottles, etc. Also in the morning before taking bath, I was made bald, all my hair was shaved and removed from the body. Everyone was waiting when my number will come for operation. All the relatives were waiting outside the ward in the corridor. There were many many emergency patients who were operated first and I was kept back. The whole day I was on fast and was hungry again, looking at the situation, my aunt (Kunda mami) from Wadala went to doctors and nurses and asked, "When will our Suhas's number come? He is not OK; on fast and hungry whole day. Quickly do the operation. We care for him!" Pappa came under tension as she directly spoke with the doctors and nurses. But doctors told her reason about the serious patients operations. Pappa thought that doctors and nurses might get angry because of such incident but the doctors didn't. I came to know that my operation was again postponed today also on tomorrow. I was very happy because I was very hungry and very thirsty. I was waiting to eat food and drink water. I had simple dinner in the night. I tried to sleep then. But I was restless due to tension. "What will happen? How will I face it?" I was missing my friends." Has anybody informed them about my health? Like these many questions were coming in my mind. In that situation I had slept and pappa, mummy and maushi were beside my bed whole night. That night Dr. Amit Mahore sir came again and told us, "Don't let him eat now! And his operation is tomorrow morning!" He said and went out of the ward. Sunday being holiday, then also Doctor told us to be ready. This made us more tensed. Next moment mummy, pappa informed everyone about my operation on Sunday morning. An emergency condition had started in mummy-pappa's life now. At that time everyone was thinking what next will happen! Sun rised of the Sunday 20th July, 2008. Pappa waked me early in the morning and because of the queue/line for bath and toilets Maushi (Surekha) brought geyser hot water full bucket for me to take bath. She gave information to my mummy about the use of geyser as mummy was unaware of its use. I was ready and was sitting on the bed. Pappa, mummy and maushi (Surekha) were giving me confidence. Pappa had made me calm by telling me "it's a minor operation." He had made my mind, before operation itself, hard, strong and fearless. So I was confident and tension free. What so ever happens, I was ready to face it. But pappa was much more in tension.

His mind was tensed but he didn't tell anyone, not a single person about my critical condition and operation. Mummy was stronger from her mind. "Whatever the doctors will do will be the best for me", was her feelings and she was saying those. This was because no one was able to do anything except doctors. Whatever happens, facing the truth and the situation, she decided to trust doctors. As I had not water for 12 hours, I was thirstier. But I wasn't allowed to drink a single drop of water also. After some time Dr. Amit Mahore came in the ward. Ward boys also came with the stretcher. It was 10'O clock in the morning. Dr. Amit Mahore asked me "Is everything OK?" I said,"Can I come walking to the operation theatre?" He replied" It's OK then, come!", and I met everybody. All relatives had come. I met mummy. I touched her feet and took her blessings. She kissed my forehead and said, "Go and come!" I met my didi (Samiksha). I hugged her. I met pappa also. Outside the ward I met my uncles, my mama's and maushi (Surekha), my cousin Mayur (Mahendra Mama's son) was also present that time and I met him too. While getting out of the ward, my doctor Dr. Amit Mahore sir was walking ahead and behind him showing hand to everyone, waving hand to everyone I was walking as if nothing had happen to me. Everyone was literally looking at me. This was the greatest peak of my self-confidence. Mayur was coming running behind me carrying two bags both in his hands with medicines. Everybody was looking at me. After entering O.T. (operation theatre), they told me to lay on the stretcher. Afterwards it was Air Conditioned (AC) so I was feeling cold and started shivering. They put blankets on me. Nearby my uncle (Ravindra) was standing. I enquired to him about where is pappa?" "He is down to bring medicines" he replied. Next moment pappa came, and kissed my hands and said, "Nothing! It's small, Doctors will take it out, don't worry!" saying this he relaxed me, and supported me and calmed me. I showed hand to Anna (Ravindra Uncle) and Mayur and doctor took me inside the main O.T. The room of O.T. reminded me about the O.T. shown in Hindi Bollywood movies. It was same as I had seen. Above the bed, there was a big focus light, light was there on the wall also and Air Condition (A.C.) was full. The nurse told me to close my eyes and go to sleep. I did accordingly and went to sleep. (Condition outside the O.T when my operation was going on – told by my mummy pappa and others afterwards.)

At the same time at my house my Grandmother (pappa's mother) and my 3rd No. uncle's wife Geeta kaki and neighbours came together and lighting the candles and agarbattis prayed the God for me. In the next building at my mama's house (Dilip) my mami (Dakshata) and their children (Dwitesh and Diksha) and my mummy's sick mother were praying, too. After giving the news of my operation the society building meeting was ended. Sunday was a holiday so everyone was at home. When we were staying at Bandra before, the neighbours (Telgu people) were also praying the God for me. At Mahim in my mummy's brother's house (Mama) Dnyandev and his family were praying to the God. The neighbours there were also praying (Telgu people). Doctors told my pappa to make stand someone near the operation theatre window. For the operation procedure, my mama Dilip and 4 No. uncle Chandramani donated their blood.

To take immediate medicines, pappa was at the ground floor medical. 2nd no. uncle Ravindra was standing near the O.T. window. When any doctors showed signal to him, he would call one person who was standing in the corridor and that person went down in the medical and give the medicines to the person and it reached again in the O.T. room. This co-ordination was required. In this my mama's son Mayur was running up and down. The gallery outside of the O.T. and ward was crowded and outside of ward was crowded only by my relatives. It was Sunday and as everyone was getting news, they came to see me. All relatives were giving confidence to my mummy. All ladies were around my mummy. They were telling mummy to have lunch. But mummy said "Only after the operation is complete, she will have the food. She was giving strength to my didi (Samiksha). Same time my friends Prathamesh Gharat, Dr. Prashant Ghorpade and Nikhil Kamble were taking news about my operation from Dilip mama on the phone. Our building society's Chairman Mr. Jagdale Baba, Treasurer Mr. Mohanty and Secretary Mr. Prakash Niwate Sir finished the meeting and had reached K.E.M. Hospital to see me. But the relatives and everybody who came were not able to see me because my operation was going on. When a patient is brought out of the ward for operation to O.T. his all things are shifted out and the bed is made empty. So Samiksha didi was sitting next to the bags of clothes and other things. Everyone was coming to meet my mummy. Naveeta mami and her children also Mamta mami and her children were present there.

In the O.T., I was kept on the chair. My neck was kept straight in a stand. This was because my operation was on the backside of my head and it wasn't possible in sleeping position. As my operation was critical, they had taken it on Sunday from 10 a.m. in the morning till 4 p.m. in the evening. My operation was over. Mayur immediately went down to my Pappa and told that "operation is completed"! Then pappa came near operation theatre and everyone gathered there. After some time doctor called my uncle (Ravindra) near and same time I was being shifting to I.C.U. Ward. That time I was sense conscious and doctor asked me showing fingers "Who is he?" I replied "He is my Uncle". I said "Thank you doctor!" to Dr. Amit Mahore sir. He was totally surprised and felt nice. Pappa called my uncles and mamas to lift me and put me on the ICU bed from the stretcher. There were one or two patients in the ICU with me. But I wasn't able to see them. Anesthesia effect was now slowly decreased and I was feeling pain. I was feeling the tight stretch because of the operation on my neck, back head. I couldn't bear the pain. I was restless. Pappa was coming in intervals and was showing keep confidence, cheering me up by his hands actions. Uncle, aunty and relatives were observing me from outside because nurses were sitting in the Ward room ICU. Pappa told all the relatives to go back home and only some people were there. My Pappa, mummy, 2nd no. Uncle Ravindra Anna, Mayur, Maushi, mamas and few relatives stayed for the night in the K.E.M. hospital. It was night now. I began to get thirsty! My throat was dry and I was whispering water! Water! Now and then. But doctors had warned my uncle Ravindra anna not to give me water by action. That time the nurse told him to give me a t-spoon of water only. I again and again started shouting asking water. The nurse got angry irritate and sent my uncle Ravindra anna out of ICU ward. Then also I was shouting and asking for water. To avoid me, nurses played songs on their cellphone and kept "Bhakti Geet",

Religious Songs! They were not paying attention to me, I felt and I was angry at that moment. I was asking for my pappa also to my uncle (Ravindra). "Where is pappa?" Has he taken blanket while sleeping?" I was asking these questions to uncle Ravindra Anna and also asking water. This was funny! I was sweating because of the oxygen mask on my face. So I was removing it now and then. The 12 hours after the operation went extreme. Nothing was in my hand at that time. My back was warmed up due to sleeping in that same position. That time my bearing capacity was crossing the limit. When uncle (Ravindra) helped me, I slowly got up a bit and to give air to my back. He was slowly moving hand on my back. I was thinking "when will these 12 hours would go!" I was frequently asking "How much time more I have to be here? When I will be taken out?" I didn't know when I slept in the restless condition of mine. I was kept in the I.C.U. whole night. Outside O.T., my uncles and mamas were sitting with crowd, the doctors and the staff shouted at them. Ravindra and Chandramani uncle one by one in intervals came to see me and go. Mummy, Maushi (Surekha), Mayur, Uncle Chandramani appa were sitting outside the 10 No. Ward with the luggage, bags etc. Mummy didn't sleep whole night. She was awaken and sitting. It was because the whole night patients who were dead, their dead bodies were taken out and that was the only way to go and come to the lift or elevator. Ward boys hardly stopped and were pushing the wheel stretchers with the dead body and passing from the gallery. Beside there was Ward No.9 of viral fever and etc. patients ward. It was full and had no empty beds so patients were kept on the ground. Mummy was getting scared of the hard sound of the stretchers. Mayur who also sleeping was getting disturb by the same. At last he too got up and sat with mummy. Beside them was uncle Chandramani appa. It was an unforgettable night which went. No one can forget it. Next morning 21/07/2008, I was brought in ward No.10 from the I.C.U. I was lifted from the stretcher and was kept on the bed. Every one met me. Relatives who stayed for the whole night went in the morning. Mummy also went to Mahim home, became fresh and came back soon with my mami (aunty) Navneeta. Surekha maushi remained home as mummy told her. Samiksha didi was in the last year of her graduation(T.Y.B.A.) in the Ruparel College, Matunga Road,

Mumbai. She was told to continue her college and studies and to be brave by our pappa . Daily she met me in the hospital and travelled from Mira Road home. She also was worried. After I was brought in the ward, many relatives started coming to see me. I had little eaten food in the afternoon. My saline was on. My guru and Karate Coach, Pravin Shukla Sir came to see me. From our Mira Road Society Mr. Arvind Pawar from Chintan I and Mr. Ananda Kamble from Chintan 3 came to see me. My friend Prashant Ghorpade's elder sister Boby tai had come to see me. Prakash mama and Seeta Bhosle aaee had also come to see me. Prerena, Staveer, Attya, Rachana Aunty (2 No.) Sangharsh, Bharat etc also came to see me. As she was old my paternal grandmother (Devki Aaee) didn't come to see me. Sangharsh, Bharat had brought flower bouquet for me. I had a nice chat with Aaee (Pappa's mother) for a while on mobile. Before the nurse would shout, mummy called all of them out of the ward. Those who were coming to see me in the hospital were shocked looking at me and my condition. It was because they were seeing such condition probably first time and we also were experiencing it for the first time. What had happened with me had never happened with anybody before. Nobody had any experience about brain surgery and condition after the surgery. It was evening and so many relatives and friends had come to meet me. After, the time was finished, security men came whistling in the ward and warned everyone to empty the ward. Then it was cleaning time. The floor was cleaned with wet duster. That time only one relative was allowed to be in the ward with the patient. The relatives were not allowed to meet their patients who came after the time was over. At 7'O clock in the evening dinner came in the ward. Because of the security everyone who were scattered and hidden then came back again to me. Hospital made food arrangements every lunch, dinner, milk, biscuits in the morning. I was hungry for 2 days. I ate hospital's food for my dinner that evening. It was simple, boiled, no taste, no spicy and no salt. Still I ate it. I woke in the night in between my sleep. Both uncles (Ravindra and Milind) were there. I told them that "I am hungry?" One of them asked the nurse can they give apple? She said fine. But the problem was the Knife. There was no Knife. At around 12 a.m. in the night. I decided to eat apple directly. When grabbed it with my teeth, it pained at my stitches at back head's sensations in operated place occurred suddenly. It was pressured bit. Then also I ate the whole apple because of hunger. The bite taken by me was certainly painful. Afterwards when I was sleeping down suddenly I remembered an old song I liked. "Na Zhatko Julfase Pani". It was sung by my favourite playback singer "Md. Rafi". In the morning I told about this to pappa and mummy. They were totally surprised at that time! Instead of bath, mummy took a wet cloth / handkerchief / towel and wiped my body. After some time medical doctor students and trainees nurses came to take information in the ward and else to practice. All were of my age. I spoke in English with everyone who came to check me. Then pappa and uncle (Ravindra) took me to the physiotherapy room. Doctor did and took my little exercise and physical activity. Nurses in the morning time were young, good looking and fair. Their behavior was also nice towards the patients. They were trying to make understand the patients their complaints and medicines on them. Some were well experienced and senior nurses. They were very strict and well disciplined. They kept a keen watch on each and every patient. Giving tablets, giving injections and checking blood pressure. These works they did whole day one by one. I was taking experience of these things. As the patients were more I was told, I will be discharged after three days. You can go home, they (doctors) said but those were rainy days in Mumbai and we were staying far from KEM hospital. So we requested to Dr. Amit Mahore sir to extend our staying at K.E.M. hospital. Then after five days I was ready to go home. Pappa had made arrangements for me. Sachin Pawar (Murtavadkar) my mama's cousin brother had charity trust's ambulance in K.E.M. Hospital. He became ready to take me to Mira Road. Dilip mama, Rahul mama, Mahendra mama, Mummy, pappa all were with me. Those were rainy season days and there were pot holes on the highway road. So the ambulance was driven slowly and steadily. In between, it was raining continuously and road problem was the issue. I was lying on the bed in the ambulance as my bandage was still on the operated back head.

To avoid any type of risk, I was made to sleep on one side. I could hear everything. Voice of rainfall, traffic of vehicles and their horns.

When our ambulance came to the main highway, it took speed. It was morning time and way was open towards Mira Road free road. When we came to Haatkesh inside the main highway, due to the bad road, ambulance took half an hour to reach our building. Here there were many pot holes and for my sake ambulance came slowly. I was made to get up from the stretcher now. Slowly catching pappa and others I was made to stand. Slowly I climbed up stairs catching pappa and others came in front of our house door. I was brought home safely at last. Sachin Pawar who was ambulance driver had to go back. So he and Rahul mama had little food. Didi had kept house clean and made everything ready. Geeta kaki had helped Samiksha didi to cook food that day. After my lunch neighbours came to see me. "Its all your blessings and regards", I was saying. That day I had my dinner at 7'O clock in the evening according to the hospital's time. It was necessary to follow their rules. Everybody was happy. I was also happy and cheerful. Next day my 3 No. uncle Milind and aunty Geeta kaki went at their house beside our building itself. We had no cable attached to our T.V. set. I was finding difficulty in watching only one National channel and limited programmes. I told my mummy, "Please attach able connection to our T.V. set for me". Next day cable connection was joined. Didi was going to her college and pappa also started going to his school. I got bored sitting at home. Dilip mama came in the morning daily. I asked him about my sick grandmother's (Mummy's mother) health. When mummy went in the evening at their place, she would ask about my health to her and enquire. After 10 days they had called us to remove the stitches. So we went to KEM Hospital on the 2nd floor, Ward No.10, neurosurgery ward. I was called near table and Chairs where the doctors and nurses sit. They cut and pulled the stitches one by one and removed them by a catcher like instrument. We were to wait for a while and we stayed out of the ward. On the place of the stitches, marks and spots of the stitching were seen there. Marks were appeared and on some stitches points blood also came out. They cleaned and told us to clean it and put bandage on the back side of my head. Give him bath and clean it with Dettol". After meeting my surgeon doctor Dr. Amit Mahore sir told us and we returned to Mira Road again by taxi. Pappa was more alert now. He grasped the instructions given by my doctor and followed it strictly and told everyone the same including me. Mummy followed all the instructions strictly for me. Pappa helped me in the bathroom to take bath with Dettol Soap and washed and cleaned the place where doctors had told accordingly. He put 2-3 times Dettol Soap on the stitches area. I was cleaned up after 10 days with a normal bathing. Pappa had given me shower. I had food according to the hospital time that evening and my daily routine began again. In early morning sunlight, fresh atmosphere and in pure air I started walking, roaming and sitting in the complex garden with Dilip mama and my mummy. Having meal on time, taking tablets regularly, this was going on. In between, my friends called me to know how my health was. Close relatives also dialed me. From K.E.M. Hospital, my brain tumour and its tissues were sent to TATA Memorial Hospital Parel for testing. Today we were going to TATA Hospital Parel Mumbai get the report of that brain tumour. So mummy, pappa and me went to TATA Hospital with Dilip mama, 2 no. Uncle (Ravindra anna) also came there. Dr. Tejpal Gupta told pappa about my brain tumour that it is not a malignant cancer stage brain tumor. It's a normal tissues benign brain tumour. Pappa became happy. Then he met Dr. Rakesh Jalali sir, head of Radiation and Oncology department Tata Hospital. He gave pappa information about the radiation and its types. He said, "We can give 2 types of radiations to Suhas (1) Traditional Regular Radiation and (2) New 50% General and 50% S.C.R.T. radiation. Pappa asked him about the second type of radiation. He said "We are giving this type of radiation to 200 patients and they are for research. This type of radiation will give new results and help us for more research. Pappa said, "What you feel better, secure and profitable for Suhas, give him that type of radiation". Then Dr. Rakesh Jalali sir gave a form to pappa to fill my information and signed it. Then I got 124 as my trial case number from the 200 patients of the SCRT type of radiation. My TATA Hospital's file number was CD-16836. My file was made, after that they gave me date of appointment for MRI. Then we returned back to Mira Road. While coming pappa took my favourite "Kandi Peddhas" Sweets from "Ramnath Bakery" at Bandra. He took more purposely. Pappa was a bit tension free now because my brain tumour was a general 1st stage benign tumour and was Cancer Free. "Pappa gave this good news to all at home and gave sweets to them. Then we had a discussion about my radiation. Going from Mira Road to TATA Hospital, Parel by taxi regular was painful for me and also expensive for us, long route and travelling by local train was not possible for me. So we decided to stay with Dnyandev mama, Deepali, Ņamrata, Nitesh, Navneeta Mami and Surekha Maushi at Mahim. My M.R.I. date came. The sun rised and early morning we reached TATA Hospital by taxi. We had bags with us. Pappa made us to sit at one place and he went to give my file number and previous MRI scans to the doctors. There my name was called and I was taken in the room to do my MRI. After that K.E.M. and TATA doctors had meeting on my case and they decided to give me 30 days of radiation. Pappa was informed about this. Before starting my radiation they took size of my head, neck and face. That time we came to know that, it was a helmet like plastic cover / net for protection (white colour) of our face, eyes, ears and etc. from the atomic rays. Where it's necessary, only and only there the radiation was given with a particular intensity, pattern and amount only so that the tissues and roots of the brain tumour would burn, destroy and not to grow again. It was like if a tree branch cut, again it grows, but if the cut part of the tree branches its roots are burnt and destroyed, then it never grows again. Its growth is stopped. After and while the radiation is given I faced many side effects. It trouble and destroys us physically. My eyes remain red until my radiation was finished. A certain type of smell (nausea) I felt in my throat, burning feeling in my body. My head became more hot / warm. Feeling of nausea (feel of vomiting). I felt weakness in my body and tired. My hair were lost backside where the radiation was going on. I had lost hunger. I had lost taste of my tongue. My body remained warm from inside. I was always getting burning smell. I also had skin allergy. Like these many more things were happening. The above experiences were unexpected for us. We had never thought of these side effects at all. I was given radiation's date and time. That was from 18/09/2008 and time was 2.30 p.m. in the afternoon. I also was given radiation token No. 4259. That was my first day of radiation. We had reached early there. Radiation room was in the basement, means below the ground floor i.e. 1st floor. Pappa met the doctors. Dr. Rakesh Jalali sir, Dr. Shashikant and other doctors were present there. Also there were technicians present who were going to handle the machine. Mummy and me, and 2 No uncle Ravindra Anna, we all were sitting at the waiting room on the ground floor. That time pappa brought me down to the basement. My number came for the radiation. I came in the common room of radiation area. There was a big oval shape machine. There was a bed to lie down. One T.V. also was there in that common room. Share market channel was being displayed in mute. I was told to go to the toilet and finish urine. I was told to remove my footwear. I was stable in mind. Then they lay me down in sleeping position on that bed. Then my size glass box was kept around my head so as my face was in the glass box. The helmet like plastic cover net which was made for me by my size was put on my face so tightly that it pressured my eyes, lips, ears, nose, mouth, chicks and whole face. My face was forcefully pressed up. I was not able to breathe properly. Still I was bearing every pain. I was telling them to take out the net / mask out but as it was the first day and they had to set up machine, set up target points of radiation, so it was taking time, they were saying me. After they finished and completed the settings, and target points the other room lights were off and it was dark and blackout. I was alone inside and pappa was outside. The technicians were also handling the machine from outside the room. At perfect target points radiation was given me the first time, but I felt tired and water dripped from my eyes. I had made up my mind to overcome all the hurdles and come out of this situation. They decided to give radiation regularly to me from now. After the first radiation "I vomited out yellow water". So they told us that 30 days radiation will be given to me. We had decided to stay at Mahim home. My sick maternal Grandmother Mahim aai Ranjana (Mummy's mother) was now shifted to Mira Road at Dilip mama's house from Mahim as it was a one room and a kitchen and the space was less. Dnyandev mama and his family, Surekha maushi and we stayed there for more than 30 days. Samiksha didi would also come at Mahim. So it was not comfortable for my sick maternal Grandmother (Mummy's mother) and she was not able to walk freely outside and inside also. Houses of Mahim are of Chawl system slums and the toilet was common and outside. Water pipe tap line was also common there and outside. We were facing this difficulty also.

Pappa's school "Anuyog Vidyalay" was at Khar (East). So early morning he got up and got ready and attended his school. In the afternoon when pappa came we had our lunch and we went to TATA hospital. Ravindra Anna uncle was also coming from Bandra at TATA hospital during the radiation period on my call. I would phone him and call him there. There in TATA hospital, different types of patients were sitting in the common waiting room. Their body had different kinds of marks and black colour skin appeared because of radiation. Because of hair fall, many patients tied scarf cloth to their heads. Our mind went still looking at the patients with tubes in their nostrils and mouth! I decided to fight and come out safely from this situation. I was ready in my mind to face whatever situation comes. Many of them told their experiences about what to eat, drink and what to avoid during the radiation period. The doctors also guided us about this. From small children to old age people, from male to females, all kinds of people came there to take radiation and chemotherapy. We were observing. Mummy, Pappa and Uncle Ravindra Anna were always with me during my radiation. Each of one, once Samiksha didi, Navneeta mami, Deepali and Namrata on separate days had come to TATA hospital to see me how the radiation was given to me. Meantime, Dr. Rakesh Jalali sir found "Hydrocephalus" (water) at the brain tumour area of my brain during radiation. He told pappa about it. Pappa asked him "Will the radiation be complete successfully or no" Dr. Rakesh Jalali sir said "Yes, but a shunt must be put in his body". We didn't know what's shunt. He only told pappa about this. A thin tube is put in the brain/head from back side of head neck muscle, stomach and is gone to the urinary bladder. The water which gets collected in the brain area is passed through the SHUNT TUBE to the urinary bladder by this tube called shunt tube. My radiation was going on. Same time I was facing side effects of the radiation. My eyes were red, A typical smell came of a burning wire, I felt hot, heat and warm from inside my body. My skin reacted and had torn slightly at some parts. I had started eating Ice-cream so I felt bit cool. I had coconut water 4 to 5 times a day. How difficult the days those were, totally different, that time. My radiation was completed. They took a post radiation MRI and told pappa that radiation was successfully done. Now we were ready to go back to Mira Road. Dnyandev mama,

Navneeta mami, Surekha maushi, Deepali, Namrata, Nitesh (bawa) and everybody in Mahim had faced problem because of me and bear it for me. It was a test for everyone. After coming to Mira Road, there was again a question in front of me about adjusting here. Travelling by taxi was the most difficulty I had to face during follow-up to hospital. In the morning time Dilip mama came with me for making me walk. As days went, I was finding difficult to balance myself. Day by day the problem of my walking became serious. I got tired soon. After taking few steps I got tired and I started sitting more. Mama came under tension looking at my condition. He told mummy, "He is not willing to walk; He gets tired soon and sits down, what's this?" There was no way to find what issue was going on with me. My urine control had decreased and I was finding difficult to make myself wait for urine. When I felt to go for urine, before reaching the toilet I was unable to control it and my clothes were getting wet. In the night my bed, bed sheets were getting wet because of me. Mummy pappa had to clean it all and pappa cleaned me up. Our sleep was disturbed because of this. All were tensed and confused. We went for follow-up to TATA hospital. There Dr. Rakesh Jalali sir told us to meet Dr. Dattatraya Mujumdar, neurosurgeon at K.E.M. hospital. We met Dr. Dattatraya Mujumdar sir and he told that its fine and gave tablets. After coming home, same problem was going on. No one could understand anything. Again mummy pappa and Samiksha didi decided to take me TATA hospital. Next morning because of traffic problem we went early. We got no traffic and we were before time. So mummy, pappa and didi decided to take me at K.E.M. hospital at first. There my surgeon Dr. Amit Mahore sir himself was there at OPD. He saw me. He checked me. He told me to show how I walk. I told him that I get tired while walking early and soon. "We will see further!" He said and we were about to go. But that moment mummy told the doctor about one thing she remembered. She told him, "He has no control on his urine." As soon as Dr. Amit Mahore sir heard this he gave reference note to do a C.T. Scan of brain immediately and bring to him. We first had breakfast and then did my C.T. Scan. We got it and we went to the 2nd floor Ward No. 10 of K.E.M. hospital and stood outside in the gallery waiting for Dr. Amit Mahore sir. He came, went in the cabin room, saw the C.T. Scan and told the nurse to admit me immediately. This time pappa decided to keep this news in family only. Mahendra mama (Bhayandar) had a friend of him in their society named Babaji Pawar who was working in K.E.M. hospital. By his efforts, I got a separate room in the ward itself where I was admitted. I was really happy to get a special room. But this created a problem further. I wished to eat "Dahi wada" (Curd and Vegcorn). Firstly it was chilled and secondly as it was sweet and tasty and yummy one. I ate both the vadas. And suddenly a "fit" came. Then I went unconscious. 2 to 3 minutes what happened I was unaware. But when I became conscious suddenly, at that time, doctors, mummy, pappa were shouting and screaming. All were running and the atmosphere was tensed. Then I was shifted to the ward near the nurses table as they would keep watch on me. Dnyandev mama had brought "Chinese Bhel" for me. But I didn't eat that. After this critical situation, everyone became alert. Doctors decided to do my operation as soon as possible. This time instead of going walking to the O.T., I went on the stretcher laying down. Before that in the night of 12-12-2008 all the relatives went home. Mummy and pappa were only there with me. Doctors told to take Chest X-ray. I was not in the condition that I could walk. So pappa went and brought a wheel chair for me. Both mummy pappa made me sit on the wheel chair and took me to the X-ray department on the first floor by lift. Then we went to M.R.I. department and did my M.R.I. We all really suffered a lot. Mummy pappa were tired.

When in the morning, I was taken in the O.T. the medicine which were necessary during the surgery were not available in the medical. Uncle Ravindra Anna had gone down to bring those. But the shunt tube which Dr. Amit Mahore sir had given in writing was not available. No mobile phone was getting connected with uncle. "Heat in mouth" situation it was! My operation was completed and after 3 hours. I was brought to the ward directly. I was swollen fully. As air went in my body I was shivering of cold.5-6 blankets were on my body to cover me. I was looking like an astronaut who was gone packed with space uniform and my face was only open. That was 13/12/2008. I was on the bed and doctors came to round and see me and go. I was paying attention to what they were talking. "Shunt

VP tube is put in! Now its fine!" Hearing this I was restless. Outside part is placed inside my body. Slowly I came to know and understood.

In simple language, a tube was put in my head / brain and body.Dr. Amit Mahore sir came out from the O.T. and asked mummy, pappa, "How strong his neck is! My steel shunt passer rod broke into his neck muscle during the surgery operation". Pappa told him, "Because of Karate practice it has become so strong!" That whole day I rested sleeping. Next day "Namita (namu) from Worli (our close relative) had her wedding. Pappa told Samiksha didi to attend the marriage ceremony taking Deepali and Namrata there. Night of 13/12/08 went painful. Next morning 14-12-2008 I got up. Pappa had gone to bring breakfast. Mummy was not near me. I asked a nurse and she told me, "Mummy is coming". I was laying down on bed. Both Pappa and Mummy came. My swollen body was reduced compared to yesterday. But from yesterday itself all of them were looking yellow yellow to me. The world also was looking yellow. I got its answer. After having 2 bread slice and tea again I went to sleep. Doctors were not yet come for the round. It was 11 a.m. and hospital lunch started to distribute it. The food was boiled and tasteless and without salt. Because of hunger I was eating it. I was made to sit on the bed and food was brought in the plate by mummy for me. Both pappa, mummy were beside me. I had to eat the food. Half of my meal was finished and suddenly Dr. Amit Mahore sir came there. "Come on! Come on! get up and stand! Now walking !without taking any support!" We just kept silence for a moment. "I just complete my round and come, till then you finish your food!" Dr. Amit Mahore sir told me and he went. I was purposely having my food slowly. I finished eating and doctor also came back. Dr. Amit Mahore sir told me to stand up by my own. I was literally afraid. Taking support of the bed, I managed to stand alone. He had removed my urine bag just before only. "Now you have to walk alone!" he said. Slowly I was stepping forward and was afraid. Suddenly I lost balance and pappa caught me. Doctor shouted, "Let him try to balance himself!" Making my mind strong, I was one by one stepping forward. I was walking similar to a small child who tries many times to walk, falls down and again walk. How a calf of a cow immediately after birth tries to stand and walk, similarly I was doing so. I was walking slowly. Dr. Amit Mahore sir said, "Take speed and walk". "Good !Right ! See up in front and walk. I was looking down at my legs and walking. "Does anyone walk looking down?" He shouted to me. "Look in front and walk as all do!" He was telling me. I was trying and practicing to walk. I walked whole ward and now stopped. I went near my bed. To get fearless, we have to face the fear! I had a lesson from this. Mahendra Mama, Mamta mami, Mayur, Sukeshni and Ragini came to see me from Bhayander. I showed them how I was able to walk now and stood outside the ward where the gallery was. All the atmosphere, surroundings and sky was looking normal. Then I understood that ward was coloured recently. I was happy. Outside on the tree ,there was a Koyal (cuckoo) bird. It was sounding "Kuhoo Kuhoo"! I too whistled and made same sound loudly. Hearing my whistle it was responding me. I was happy. I did urine there, and I was about to do toilet also. I told pappa and he immediately took me inside. But I had already done toilet in the pant. Instead of going near the bed, pappa took me to the bathroom to clean me and bath me. We finished and wearing towel to me, pappa was bringing me and near my bed a red belt senior officer aged nurse shouted loudly on us. "Is this time to have bath? What's this on towel?" Mummy stood on her place with and bucket full of water. Pappa also was angry on her but didn't say anything. But another nurse told pappa "Leave it". Then with cold water, I was cleaned and given bath and taken me to my bed. Samiksha didi, Deepali and Namrata had quickly returned from Namita's wedding without having food there. Everyone was present here at K.E.M. hospital. Pappa again told me to walk. I had just taken two steps and suddenly something poked in my leg foot and went in and blood came out. When seen, it was sharp glass broken injection bottles which were thrown in the dustbin, some broken pieces were outside on the floor and I happened to walk on that way and that had happened. Nurses in the ward were told and warned about this.

According to the doctors, shunt VP surgery is a minor surgery operation. But it was for them. Not for us. When boils occur on the body skin, water gets collected in it, same in brain surgery in the place of the brain tumour area, water is generated naturally. This hydrocephalus water hurdles the smooth functioning of brain. If it gets collected and touched near small brain which is backside of our head (in my case) it creates pressure and pressurizes our brain and ultimately our whole body. It also disturbs our nerve system, balance. All our activities go slow. We loose control on our body. In my case this happened so many times. My control on urine was decreased. And also one can be unconscious. The food like carbohydrate, starch, roots, brinjal etc. when I ate and eat now, hydrocephalus is generated in my brain tumour operated area. It pressures my eyes, face and my movements go slow. This was the reason my control on the urine went minimum. I remember during my radiation period, I was unable to eat normal food. I had lots of fried potato chips which was dipped in channa water and made bhaji. I had those with chappatis. The shunt VP surgery is different. The hydrocephalus (water) which pressures the brain, it drips but it is very slow. But to make the water going process faster a shunt VP tube is put which is from the head till the urinary bladder. The tube is flexible. This tube is similar to our blood carrier artery veins which we find in our hands hard and flexible. During my shunt VP tube surgery, my surgeon Dr. Amit Mahore made a hole in my head from the top, then made a cut at my right side neck muscle and a cut on my right side stomach beside the belly. Then he put in a steel metal rod called shunt passer from my head to the neck where cut was there. Means he created a way for the flexible tube called Shunt VP to enter my head. Then he inserted the tube from the steel rod /passer from my head till my neck. Similarly he did till the tube went till my urinary bladder. It's like when the ocean is digged, to get fuel and natural gas it is similar. In this way surgery is done my pappa told me this, later years.

I was expecting discharge on 15-12-08 and they gave. But before leaving the hospital, Dr. Amit Mahore came to meet us from O.T. itself in the operation gloves, gown, cap and mask and instructed pappa mummy. They were having lunch sitting near between two beds. He asked" Ready to Go?" Got discharge papers?" Pappa answered "Yes, Doctor". "Now everything is fine, only have to take good care." He said to us. Saying this he again went in the O.T. Me, mummy, pappa and uncle Ravindra anna left my hands. My hand was swollen I was walking alone without any body's support. I thanked everybody in the ward including nurses and ward boys also and went down by elevator. I walked till taxi and went to mama's house at Mahim. In hospital itself I had worn adult dipper and had come to Mahim. Now I had control on my urine and I could control it for longer time too. While coming from Parel and Dadar T.T. bridge I found everything new. Seeing the skyscrapers, traffic and vehicles, my mind was scared. Also I viewed the sunset after couple of days. While coming, pappa told he wants to go out for urgent work and told mummy to let someone come on the bus stop. She gave me support and catching her slowly and steadily, we came home. It was a nice moment. I remembered my radiation days. We went for a walk during my radiation and I knew now also how to go. I was ready to eat Vada Pav, Chicken lollypop, soup and much more. I ate all these during my radiation and also ice-cream which I had lot. Everyone in my family came to see me at Mahim. Also my pappas's school teachers, relatives, Bhosle family and my friends.

My swollen body after my operation slowly reduced. But the hand where saline IV was attached that part was still swollen till now. After applying ointment also the hand was swollen as it is. In the night pappa again applied ointment to my hand. By mistake while talking it touched my shirt I was wearing. Deepali and pappa saw that there was a small (dishpot) plastic paper on my hand. When blood is given, that time a plastic tape sticker is put on the injected part that plastic paper was there. The ointment which was applied last 2days by pappa was not at all going in my skin because of this small, tiny plastic paper. If pappa had not cleaned my hand with cotton, then without knowing anything we would keep applying ointment on my hand. When we were at Mahim, I memorized phone number of my college dear friend. His name is "Abhishek More". I called and his family said that he is staying at Kolhapur Maharashtra district and gave his contact number. We were now in contact. Similarly my high school and Bandra friend Vinay Dwivedi also came to see me at Mahim. As my uncle Ravindra's anna's elder son 'Sangharsh' was studying in my school Cardinal Gracious High School, Bandra East, my uncle gave the news about my operation of brain tumour there. Every teacher was shocked knowing this news. I was "head body in 10th Std" of my school. In school as well as after my school finished (after 10th Std.) I was continuously going to Karate Class for practice and all were watching. That time my teachers met me. "But what suddenly happened to Suhas?" They had a question. My teacher Trupti Patil started crying hearing about my operation according to uncle Ravindra Anna who told me this. While travelling, teachers met Samiksha didi at Bandra station regularly and asked about my health and condition. That time "Greta Pharel", our teacher took our residential address and phone number from "Samiksha didi". After examinations soon she came to see me. I was more happy when I met her. Meeting her I felt nice. I was satisfied and felt supported by knowing someone had come to see me from my school. It was necessary to take care of my eating and drinking every day. Mummy was doing so. But I wanted to restart my college. Considering it, pappa said, "Go if it is possible for you". I started going to college for B.Sc. 2nd year at Vartak College, Vasai. Those were not my friends of last year. This was a new batch and nobody knew me and all were unknown students. I was attending lectures and practicals. So I was not able to have my food on time. I was not able to concentrate on my health care. I came home tired now. No rest, hectic schedule, getting up early in the morning, going to college without food may be little but it started again. Due to sweating lot, my electrolytes and water level decreased, dehydration started, tilting / squinting my eye balls started. It disturbed me and two images appeared. Looking at my condition and the increasing problem both mummy pappa told me to stop going to college and leaving studies too. I was doing this on my strength. After some days, the eye balls had tilted/ squinted more and my vision was blurred. It increased and two images started coming on my vision. The difference of eye balls had increased a lot. Imediately we went to K.E.M. hospital Parel. We met Dr. Amit Mahore sir and he told me to do M.R.I. Scan urgently. After that he admitted me in ward no. 10, but slowly my vision recovered and my eyeballs became straight again. Next morning, Dr. Amit Mahore sir said, "This time, I won't take any decision about operation.". I didn't take his words seriously, but I told him a thing, "I can feel hydrocephalus passing through the shunt VP tube of mine." He began to laugh and said, "One cannot feel it" and I too smiled and kept quite. In the evening I was given discharge from the hospital. I wanted to spend this day at home but was not possible. As doctors were not in the hospital their meeting on my case delayed and I was made to stay that night. But now we were at home. Doctor had made me understand that you have studied a lot. 14th standard is much. Dr. Amit Mahoresir said one phrase "Sar Salamat to Pagdi Panchaas!" This actually means if your head his secured (meaning life is secured) you can wear as many caps of different styles (you can do anything).

Coming back to Mira Road, mummy pappa and didi made me understand and pappa didi went to my Vartak College and cancelled my admission. Every month / three / six month I had to go for followup at TATA Hospital. After my radiation, I was under follow-up and was under their observation. They had given me SCRT radiation. There on place of physiotherapist Dr. Shashikant Chandanshive, a new doctor was appointed. Thereafter there was Dr. Mansi Takle. She took my physio therapy. I also went to psychologist doctor there. One was Dr. Savita Goswami and other was Dr. Lekhika. To know my condition about my brain psychology they had taken many tests which I did every 6 months. They tested me and saw my psychological, mental situation, condition and my memory, how much I can remember things, I.Q. Test (Intelligent Quotient), thinking capacity, all the time limit tests. Test of recognizing different pictures, shapes, colours. These small things also were difficult for me. My tongue had become heavy to speak fluent and speaking ability was also affected. Doctor gave me exercise and told me to practice opening lock by key by own. This was to improve my brain co-ordination ability. I found difficult putting key in the hole of the lock. They also told to extract stones out from rice grains. These small things of daily household work helped me to become used to these things and my brain became alert and working. From TATA hospital they sent us to the eye surgeon at Santacruz West referred by them only. Dr. Ajay Dudhani sir, an eye specialist and my eyes doctor now. Here also we had to go every six months. All the brain tumour patients were sent here. He had an advanced machine by which vision, sight was examined. This machine was available in few big hospitals only in Mumbai. It was computerized machine. His assistant nurse Bharti Sawant put drops in our eyes first. Then my one eye was shut closed by cotton and a tape was put on it and one eye was left open for test. In the semicircular shape of machine which was curved from inside, we had to keep our chin on the stand there and keep looking at a small red light. A trigger was given in my hand. Looking straight to the red dot, if we happen to see green light blink in the area, I had to press the trigger. All the points were called hitted strokes and then by my other eye same procedure was repeated. Then both the results were printed and Dr. Ajay Dudhani sir would see and examine the report and tell us how much my vision has improved and how it can more improve. While keeping chin on the stand, my neck pained a lot. But I had decided in my mind to come out of this situation.

After radiation and shunt VP tube surgery rashes appeared on my skin. And the inner skin surface looked blood red and was torn too. So we went to skin specialist, dermatologist Dr. Pramod Bhandari in Mira Road. He checked me and gave oinment and tablets for ten days. 2 to 3 times we had gone to him. As time will go the rashes will be cured, doctor said. I was getting better and everything was fine now. I got up on time some days, had breakfast, much on time. Some time, I got up late and timetable was disturbed then. In between I ate ice-cream, chicken lollypop from hotel. Many outside stuff I started to have, I was free. I started thinking, I am sitting home and only eating. If I work and earn then I will financially support for my family. I was told not to lift anything more than 1 ½ Kg. So I was not able to do hard work at all. So I kept silence. I didn't have outing. Doctor had told to avoid travelling long route. In Jan.2010 I went in the theatre with mummy pappa and didi to see Hindi movie "3 Idiots". That time I had put cotton balls in my ears and had worn woolen cap upto my ears. I liked the move and I enjoyed also. I had kept the move tickets for several days as a memory. Afterwards we didn't have a chance to see movie in the theatre together. Once Mayur, Samiksha didi and I went to see "Pirates of the Carabian-On the stranger Tides" in theatre. Mermaids shown were awesome, beautiful and sensitive in this movie. I felt movie O.K.! On the whole, I was pretending to be blind or like a person who lost his vision. I was workless and was eating being home. And this feeling actually was disturbing me. All were ready to go Murtavade, Chiplun, District Ratnagiri (Mummy's native place) for new house warming ceremony. Pappa had gone to (Kudli Taluka Guhagar District Ratnagiri our native place) then grandmother (his mother) before. Now I was distracted and I also decided to go village with all. I called up Dr. Amit Mahore sir and took his permission. "Yes!" he said to me. But when I asked pappa, "Don't come!" he said and I left the subject. That time, I had recorded video of my sick maternal Grand Mother (Mummy's Mother) before with Mayur's handicam. I felt nice that I showed good presence of mind. Everyone went to their respective native places that year. Mr. Prakash Pandurang Niwate Sir's family, Dilip mama, Mahendra mama, Dnyandev mama, Uncle Milind bhaee and their families also went. Samiksha didi, Surekha maushi also went with Dilip mama's private bus. Mummy and myself were only left behind. After few days one by one they returned back. I was bored. I was interested and waiting to eat Hapus (mangoes)/ Alphanso when all came. Now our house was again like house because of members presence I felt. I saw photos of village and house inauguration ceremony. I wished I could attend it also. But my health was more important I thought. I was bit careless about my diet that time, but my health was stable that period. I was reading and was writing poems that time. Our financial condition was bit improving, I felt. Samiksha didi had started teaching at degree level Ruparel College, Matunga raod, Mumbai and pappa was feeling supported by her. Mummy was also happy. I told Mayur to bring his handicam and told that we will shoot maternal Grandmother's (Mummy's mother) life. I pointed out several questions to ask her about her experiences in her life. We went at Dilip mama's house. I asked each and every question and Mayur recorded all the answers of her life. As I was feeling better and better, I started thinking about job, work. I felt if I work, I will support financially my home. And I started searching ads in newspapers regarding job. Pappa was observing the situation silently. I didn't feel I was doing any hurry, but I was in a hurry. I saw an advertisement of a corporate company in the newspaper and contacted them. The agent told me to come. Pappa and I became ready to go there. Mummy gave us chappati and vegetable in a tiffin box to have in the lunch time. In the local train while reaching there, pappa said, "We would just enquire and take experience about it. We were feeling tired because of hectic travelling. I was sweating a lot. I was tired. We reached "Ghatkopar station". I met a madam there. I told her everything about my education, staying far, my surgery operation etc. She gave me an address of a company at Mulund. She took fees Rs. 1000/- too. We came home. Pappa was silent. I was very tired. Next day we went searching the given address at Mulund. I had worn T-shirt and Trouser. In the corporate world, people wear shirt, pant and tie. I was unaware of this. We reached there. We were sweating and tired too. We were told to sit. They asked me some questions. Knowing my travelling and my problem they told that they'll contact me. Mummy gave us the tiffin which we ate at a small hotel near Mulund station. Pappa first requested them and then they permitted us. We ate the chappatis and vegetable, had water and returned home. I was sweating and so was dehydrated. Pappa told me to avoid hurry and keep patience, everything will be fine. I had searched jobs on internet also for some days. Then slowly because of sweating, dehydration increased and it affected my vision and my eyeballs were more tilted/ squinted. Mummy pappa became alert knowing my condition and made me understand that, health is more important, rest things afterwards, "Sar Salamat to pagdi panchaas", that phrase made me leave the subject of doing job. But I had a loss of my health. I had lost water, sugar, salt via sweat and it was necessary to fulfill it. And I didn't do that. In month of May, pappa took Grandmother (papp'smother) to village and brought her back in 15 days. But I was dehydrated a lot because of loose motions and it affected my vision and eyes got tilted/ squinted. We decided to go K.E.M. hospital and meet Dr. Amit Mahore sir. We called him up and he said us to come. We went and met him with my latest M.R.I. done. Because of my tilted/squinted eyeballs and vision, he told us to do a contrast M.R.I. beside the K.E.M. hospital. It look 1½ hours for that M.R.I. We had lunch there beside hotel and then we met Dr. Amit Mahore sir. He saw the scans and told us to go home. Here started a big problem. I was not able to bear pain, and resist the contrast injection given to me during M.R.I. We came back to Mira Road by taxi. It was a huge and hectic, tiring journey. Coming home I started vomitting. I was unstable now. Dehydration increased and became extremes. Pappa immediately called Dr. Amit Mahore sir and told about my critical condition. He told pappa to bring me immediately in K.E.M. hospital. That was a Sunday and my aunty (Mai attya and Mama (her husband Pramod) with their children mani and bawa (Prerna and Sthaveer) had come to discuss about the Bandra houses issue (property issue) at Mira Road. The issue had become really hot that same time. But pappa avoided the matter and decided to take me to the K.E.M. hospital. Everybody was around me leaving the lunch. When my vomits were continuously going on and in one of vomit pappa saw blood, he again called Dr. Amit Mahore sir and told him about this. Doctor said to bring me to K.E.M. hospital immediately to K.E.M. hospital. Uncle Milind bhaee went to bring taxi. Mummy, Pappa, uncle Milind bhaee and I sat in the taxi and left but my vomiting was not at all stopped.I felt unconscious. At last pappa asked Dr. Amit Mahore and he said, "admit him to a nearby hospital for that night only and make him stable, let his vomits stop, then bring him to K.E.M. hospital next morning". A honest Indian Sikh taxi driver brother was understanding the situation and told us about a hospital nearby in Mira Road. Pappa took me straight there and I was admitted there. They put-up saline glucose. I was serious and critical. When I was admitted, I was unstable and totally restless. They checked my file, reports and as per pappa's suggetion they called up a Neurosurgeon. Pappa informed relatives and immediately they came to help. Pappa mummy were under tension. They didn't know what to do. Pappa was discussing with the nursing home doctors. The neurosurgeon who came to see and check me saw the previous M.R.I. scans and said that the tumour has grown and the shunt VP tube is also not working. I had blood vomits in the house, so my critical condition made me unconscious the whole night. The neurosurgeon suggested emergency surgery. The hospital told us that there can be operation here, but won't guarantee that life would be saved. They didn't take any responsibility of further. They told they will charge Rs 1,50,000/- Pappa, mummy were into a do or die situation. They thought to discuss, think and take any decision. Mummy pappa and relatives were under tension. Pappa decided to call Dr. Amit Mahore sir once again, and told him my condition and suggestions of the neurosurgeon and private nursing home doctors. He said, "He is my patient. Bring him at K.E.M. hospital when his vomits are stopped. Only I knew his case history!" Pappa decided to follow him. We spent a night here and pappa requested the nursing home to arrange a cardiac ambulance with a doctor and a nurse to shift me to K.E.M. hospital tomorrow in emergency. Didi was at home. Aaee (Papa's mother) and Attya (Pappa's younger sister) were there. Didi completed all the household stuff and came in the night at the nursing home. Both my uncle and mama houses had sent dinner for night but nobody was in the state to have food. As soon as news that I was admitted, my Karate Coach Pravin Shukla Sir and Khushboo (his sister-in-law) had come to see me. They were boosting up Pappa, mummy and didi. Khushboo was telling mummy, "He is my brother, nothing will happen to him. You don't worry, Every one's blessings are there". A friend and his wife of uncle Milind bhaee also came to see me there. Uncle Ravindra anna also came there. But I was semi conscious and was not in the state to recognize any body. All these things now I came to know what had happened that time. Pravin Shukla Sir was with Samiksha didi and Pappa. He said, "Suhas is a fighter! He will definitely come out from this!" Pappa was boosted by these words of Pravin Shukla Sir and ahead in future Pappa kept remembering his words and kept trying. And according to his words all the things happened. That night was a black night for us. Mummy, Pappa, didi were with me. Whole night I was getting up, sitting and was again laying down on the bed. I was restless extremely. My head was paining continuously and I was pulling my hair as if my head would burst off. I was unable to bear pain. Mummy and didi were giving me support. But I was not getting rest because of my head. I was not sleeping at all. I was vomiting as I drank water. My throat had dried. Every time when I had water, I vomited it out. Mummy, Pappa and didi were tired and confused. My condition was critical. Nurse gave me an injection as doctor told her. Some time later I slept for some hours. It worked. Pappa told the private nursing home that he will pay them charges for the cardiac ambulance, a doctor and a nurse arrangement also. Pappa did all arrangements to shift me to the

K.E.M. hospital that morning. He became more resilient as he had not enough money. In this difficult situation my pappa's dear friend and our building society General Secretary, art teacher Mr. Prakash Pandurang Niwate Sir who had shown Pappa Mira Road house which he bought, came to help. He gave pappa Rs. 10,000/-. Now there was hurry to keep me in the ambulance. My file, scans, clothes bags and other things were kept in the ambulance. My uncle Milind bhaee forgot to wear his sandals in hurry and sat in the ambulance. Mr. Prakash Pandurang Niwate sir had back and hip ache that time. Still bearing the pain he came running for me. Giving the medical emergency siren on the highway, the ambulance started running to the K.E.M. hospital Parel Mumbai direction. Uncle Milind bhaee sat with driver in front seat. Mummy, Samiksha didi, pappa and Mr.Prakash Pandurang Niwate sir were at the back side with me. Pappa was crying on Niwate's Sir's shoulder. He was making pappa understand and silent. But mummy was brave and was facing the situation. Didi was afraid in her mind. What will happen? No one could understand anything. Ambulance had picked up speed. Because of traffic jam problem, ambulance was taken from "Dharavi" route/way. There also traffic jam was present. But our ambulance was moving slowly. "Cops were checking each and every vehicle. It was a police drill. In few minutes, ambulance came inside the K.E.M. hospital's gate. A message was sent to the operation theatre on the 2nd floor where Dr. Amit Mahore sir was doing surgery via intercom. As soon as he received the message, on the same dress (operation theatre gown) he came out. I was brought by elevator on the 2nd floor. I was unconscious. Looking at me he scolded pappa," You took my patient walking home and brought him back laying down!" Pappa didn't say a single word. Pappa handed me in Dr. Amit Mahore sir's hand and took a sigh of relief. Fourth time I was admitted into No.10 of neurosurgery ward. Due to severe dehydration by vomiting, I lost electrolytes salt and water level from my body to such an extent that I had fallen unconscious. I faced upper gauge problem (The upper eye lides cannot be lift up and blinked. They become heavy) Immediately my treatment was started. As soon as they got my news of admission in K.E.M. hospital, my two friends, "Abhishek More and Mangesh Chaudhari of Mahatma Phule Junior College, Bhoiwada

Parel, came running to see me. They were shocked looking at my condition. Till then I was a bit conscious now. As I was unable to see anything, my other senses were activated and worked more now. My bed was on a quite a distance from the windows of the ward. Still I was irritated by the smell smoking of cigarattes by the workers outside the building who were working. I told this to my friends also. That night went. Doctors were having meeting. Next morning we came to know, now operation is there. This time Dr. Amit Mahore sir called both my pappa and my mummy near the O.T. He asked "Is he only son of yours?". "Yes! He is only." Mummy Pappa replied. Then Dr. Amit Mahore sir said, "See, the operation is very sensitive and critical! Chance of losing life! What do I do? Paralysis can occur! Can be bedridden whole life! Means anything can happen". Pappa mummy showed faith on Dr. Amit Mahore sir. They said, "What we will do after taking him home? What we can do?" As Dr. Amit Mahore sir had said, "If we don't do his operation, his condition will remain as it is. His vision problem will also remain same." So both pappa and mummy left everything on Dr. Amit Mahore sir and signed the medical papers. As it was my third surgery there, they had charged no fees. But it was risk of life! My condition was worst. I was unconscious. In the night I was made bald. All hair on my body were removed. I was given water bath. 12th July 2011, at 10'o clock in the morning I was taken in the O.T. Taking advantage of my pappa's depressed condition and tensed situation, uncle Ravindra Anna was poking him about the Bandra property SRA-2 ABCD and was continuously saying, "I have made that, I have got that!" I have done this and that!" That was not the place and time for such an argument. Pappa mummy and uncle Milind bhaee were quietly hearing him. "People show their true behavior in the bad condition of ours", its really a true saying! It was right and fit for the situation. When the situation went across the limit, mummy shouted him and said, "Life threatening brain surgery operation of my son is going on inside and what nonsense you are talking here? Just go down!" Pappa was all alert about not letting any relative and any other friend or anybody to know about my surgery. As we had an experience of all the doctors shouting at us during first surgery. This time my operation was completed. Surgery took 6 hours. Dr. Amit Mahore sir came out.

Mummy Pappa went near him. He said, "See! I have done my duty! Rest everything depends on his recovery! I have removed 98% of the brain tumour and that to also on my risk. We don't have permission to do so, but still I have done it. No surgeon in the world can take out the remaining 2% brain tumour because it can cause a life threat". Mummy Pappa heard these very important words of Dr. Amit Mahore sir and felt, recognized the responsibility to save me and to keep me alive. This responsibility came on each and everyone present there. I was kept in the O.T. itself. Through signs, pappa called mummy in the O.T. from a transparent glass. The doctors told mummy to clean the blood spots and the blood which was fallen on my body. I can't imagine about the condition of my mummy that time. I was unconscious. Surekha maushi was with my mummy. Mummy was afraid, but in that condition she cleaned up my head wiping it with a cloth wet with warm water. She wiped blood spots. She felt supported because of her elder sister Surekha maushi. I was kept in the I.C.U. I was now free from the tumour. Today also mummy papa and didi (Samiksha) tell me what efforts the doctors, nurses and hospital take to save one patient's life, they had experienced and saw it. The upcoming 48 hours are the most important life and death hours!" Dr. Amit Mahore sir said. "If he comes out safely from it then he will win the battle, he said. Those were his words. Everybody had misunderstood that after operation everything is fine. As getting news of my operation relatives, friends started coming to see me. Teachers from my pappa's school and whole Anuyog family came to see me. Pappa had no money now. Crying while speaking on the phone, pappa told about my critical condition as well as his worst financial condition to the founder of Anuyog Shikshan Sanstha, education expert and winner of President Trophy for "Best Teacher", Mr. Satish Dattatray Chindarkar sir and asked for help. The very next moment he told pappa, "How much money you want just say the amount!" Pappa told him to send Rs. One Lakh in cash. Soon didi (Samiksha) went to Anuyog Vidyalay, Khar (E) and Mr. Chindarkar Sir gave her Rs. One Lakh, hard cash amount in her hand to save my life. She came back with the money to the K.E.M. hospital. No one was able to understand what will be the condition ahead. When my operation was going on, same time, my didi (Samiksha) was getting calls from

K.C. College Churchgate , Mumbai to give interview for the post of Asst. Professor, for Senior College to teach. She avoided many calls but atlast she took one. Prof. Rama Vishwesh madam told didi (Samiksha) to come and start teaching directly. She was senior professor in K.C. College Economics department. Didi (Samiksha) told her that "My brother's brain tumour surgery operation is going on at K.E.M. hospital. I can't come" But they were not sure. So Prof. Rama Vishwesh madam came to K.E.M. hospital; sent her driver in ward No.10 ;2nd Floor. The driver saw my condition, took the documents of didi (Samiksha) and went down and told Prof. Rama Vishwesh madam what he saw. Didi (Samiksha) informed them that she won't be able to come for next few days. They also told didi (Samiksha) that they will wait for her. This was all the day of 12th July 2011. When I was in the O.T. first , I was kept on another bed. But I was again shifted on another bed where Dr. Amit Mahore sir told. It was a restless night for all. Pappa mummy decided to have simple food. Because of extra salt the Blood pressure would rise, so they were more alert. And if they have to keep me fine, they must keep themselves fit first. Worrying all these things both were having their B. P. tablets there also in the K.E.M. hospital. It was necessary for them to keep their own health fine. My whole future was depended on them and their health. This decision became important and was the big stand of pappa mummy. Running up and down, caring for me was possible to pappa only because of that.

Next day 13th July 2011, whole Mumbai city was disturbed because it had faced Bomb blasts. All the hospital was crowded, people were running on emergency to admit the victims of the blasts which had occurred at Dadar Kabutarkhana. People with head injuries were brought to the I.C.U. where I was kept. I was again shifted out in other I.C.U. bed. There was all hurry and chaos in the hospital. All the doctors, nurses and the staff was treating the patients who were brought to the ward and I.C.U. in emergency. Pappa, mummy, didi and other relatives had kept me safe in this situation also. Some of the victims died in the hospital who were brought. Now it was a test of me and all my people. Doctors had kept an eye continuously on my health condition. I and a patient named 'Rahul' were in ICU ward.

Mummy and Surekha maushi were inside to look after me. Dr. Amit Mahore sir had told them to give him my urine colour report frequently. Dark colour, light colour, urine colour observation was going on. My throat was getting dry and I was dam thirsty. I was continuously whispering "Water! Water!". In the morning doctor came for a round. He told to keep a wet cotton ball on my lips. I was restless, thirsty and was desperate to drink water. I sucked the wet cotton with mouth and sucked all the water in it. It wasn't enough. Again I was disturbed because of thirst. Because of vomiting I was avoided giving water. When a senior nurse came, I literally snatched the bottle of water from her hand and directly drank water by my mouth. She kept looking surprisingly at me and said, "Let him drink as much water he wants to drink!"

My home relatives came in the evening to see me. Very few were present near the O.T. still the ward man warned them to go away. But pappa told everyone to stand separate keeping distance and in voice reach. So mummy, didi, pappa, Ravindra anna uncle, Chandramani appa uncle, Milind bhaee Uncle and Ravindra Prakash Suryavashi (later my brother-in-law) stood with each other separately. After sometime ward man again shouted "Who is Suhas's relative?" Pappa immediately reacted. I was suddenly restless. It was serious and in pain. Pappa was told by Dr. Amit Mahore sir that an urgent C.T. Scan is a must. "Call all your relatives!" Immediately everybody came there. I was lifted and kept on the stretcher. I was taken by an elevator to the C.T. Scan room on the first floor. I was unconscious. Mummy started crying at that time. Didi (Samiksha) had paid the C.T. Scan Fees and filled the form. Efforts again had started to save my life. Dr. Amit Mahore sir was standing outside the O.T. 2nd floor and was taking information about my C.T. Scan on intercom and mobile phone. "There is no hydrocephalus, no blood clotting. Only neumocephallus is seen", Dr. Raghu sir said from C.T. scan room. So Dr. Amit Mahore sir said, "Bring up Suhas!". He came to know why, I was so much restless. It was air in my brain area (Neumocephallus). Then they arranged curtains around me and did something. After some time I was stable. Today also we don't know what exactly doctors did on the "Neumocephallus(air in my brain) issue." That night was really a black night. My mummy was alone. Samiksha didi pappa and everybody was running for me. Late night Surekha (maushi) came there. My mummy had an emotional support. Now I was shifted to the General ward next morning. Nobody was able to understand what exactly had happened to me. Sitting beside me, if anybody would speak, I felt like they were shouting. So I indicated them to speak softly or through action. I had lost my vision / sight. My right side was paralysed. I had lost my memory. No one noticed this. Little sound also irritated me because I had lost my vision. My hearing sense had become more sensitive. The electrolytes and salt was reached at minimum level of my body. So I was continuously given Na[1] (Sodium) injections. Because of the heavy injection doses , loose motions started. Everything was on the bed. But in this condition also pappa decided to clean me, wash me alone! He put curtain around my bed and told my uncles, mama's and relatives, only to give what things he needed". He didn't give anybody to touch me while cleaning me. After few minutes again loose motions occurred and same all the cleaning process pappa would do.

Once I vomited. Then I was not given anything to eat. When Dr.Amit Mahore sir came to know about this, he got angry. He shouted "I had told you all to keep him feeding as possible. No matter vomiting happens! Go if you don't want to listen to me; I wont' come now! Don't bring him to me!" But after sometime he came to see me and had a watch. Once Samiksha didi told Dr. Amit Mahore sir, "Suhas is getting dysentery!" Hearing this, Dr. Amit Mahore sir got angry on her. He shouted, "Do you know what is Dysentery?" "If blood is in the toilet, that's dysentery. This is only loose motions!" After some time he would come for a round and looked at my condition. During brain fever, he had told pappa, mummy, didi and ward doctors, nurses to give me Crocin (Paracetamol) tablets every 4 hours. My brain fever got over now. But my sodium level was not at all rising up. Dr. Amit Mahore sir told pappa mummy, "Give him salt as much as he can from food." Hearing this both were surprised. He told to give me curd with salt and boiled eggs with salt, Juice with salt. So each day three times, one full glass curd and 2-3 T-spoons salt. Forcefully I started having it. With that 1 egg boiled 4 times a day. That egg also was with salt. Navneeta mami from Mahim started bringing food to us in the hospital of both lunch and dinner times. Mummy Pappa thought and told her to bring dried fish (salted and dried). So she prepared dry fish (salted fish) curry and brought me. Dnyandev mama, Navneeta mami, Surekha maushi, Deepali, Namrata and Nitesh bawa took lots of efforts for me and for us. Mummy Pappa and Samiksha didi's clothes were sent to Mahim. Those were washed, ironed and brought back every day. Many such small things the Mahim family did for us. 24 hours mummy, pappa and Samiksha didi were with me. Several times pappa cried looking at my worst condition. But my mummy stood strong same time. She said pappa, "Our son will be fine. Smile in front of him." So strong and supportive my mummy was. Hearing this all about her, I feel proud that I am her son. From childhood, pappa had never cleaned my urine and toilet. There might be an exception case only. But during my illness, he only was doing that and did everything and didn't allow anyone to do it. I feel proud that I am his son. Pappa, mummy told Samiksha didi to start her teaching at K. C. College. Firstly she wasn't ready to start going there, but as my health condition started improving and I became safe, she was more relaxed and comfortable and had patience and started going to K.C. College Churchgate, Mumbai from K.E.M. hospital Parel Mumbai itself. Every day, early morning at 4 a.m., mummy gave Samiksha didi water for shower in the bathroom of ladies ward. First time our Surekha maushi showed them how to use geyser. There after mummy and Samiksha didi tried to do so. I am proud of my elder sister Samiksha didi.

It was a test for all of us. It was do or die situation for all of us. Brothers of my pappa (my uncles) helped us a lot. They didn't financially helped pappa more, but on humanity basis, they did more. Lifting me up, running up and down, bringing medicines and many things. They supported us that time. Whatever had happened, Samiksha didi and I had grown up playing on their shoulders. Ravindra anna uncle went home to Virar and Bandra during night. So pappa called up Milind bhaee uncle and Chandramani appa uncle by phone to come and help us for night. Mummy Pappa should at least get few hours rest and sleep was all the intension about all this. On this basis, whole day pappa ran up and down several times for me and mummy stayed to look after me, my things and my health. In the night, my Surekha maushi also came in the hospital. This was a relief and big support for my mummy. Whole day after looking at me, running up and down, both slept in the night getting tired. They were alert during sleep also. One night mummy had a dream thought that I am thirsty and was yelling for water. She got up and came in the ward and saw that I was laying on the bed and was really whispering "Water! Water!" Both uncles Milind bhaee and Chandramani appa who came tired from whole day slept on the chair itself got awake. Then one of them put hand under my neck and I was made to drink some water. The thirst was severe because I was having large amount of salt in food and jucies to increase my sodium level. Many such incidents were occurring that time. Dr. Amit Mahore sir once came and said pappa, "He is alive! Secured! He is lucky! It's a miracle!" From these statements of Dr. Amit Mahore sir I understand that he is my GOD and saved my life; and this is my second birth! My condition was not as good as one can say. As I had no vision, my hearing sense had become more active and so I could hear subtle voice like a big noise. Mummy spoke softly, but I couldn't bear that much slow voice also. Many times I was unable to speak normal word because of I had lost control over my speech and tongue, so I got irritated. "Talk slowly", I would say via action. My condition had become like a small baby. Pappa frequently asked Dr. Amit Mahore sir, "When his vision /sight will return?" Two three times he replied in frustration "Don't ask me same question again and again and don't make curd of my brain; I told you it will take time!" I was not able to see anything, truth I would say rather. So I don't remember anything about hospital and what happened in the 9 months ahead. I heard everything from my mummy, pappa, Samiksha didi and others. Pappa had taken decision to stay in the hospital until my life is safe and secured during this surgery operation. Pappa requested Dr.Amit Mahore sir about this. He had a keen focus on my health condition as well as whole team of him 24 hours. Now I was made to sit on the bed itself giving support. My right side was paralyzed and my body was severely affected. I had lost control on my tongue and vocal chord. My tongue had become heavy to lift. "A a b b" I was able to say hardly. I wasn't able to do anything because I had no vision, no memory, no balance. I was fully depended on others! The brain tumour was exactly where the neck and spine meet. To reach it, nerves and blood vessels of my eyes, ears, throat and oral organs which were controlled by brain had to cut off and make a way. It was very much essential to sacrifice them to save my life. Pineal Gland / Pineal body is the area of the brain tumour where it was located in the brain. The name of my tumour was "Tectal plate glioma; Pilocytic Astrocytoma; It was WHO Grade-I type of brain tumour. We just say brain tumour in normal day to day language. Ahead we were having many experiences. After 20days I was going to get a discharge, but pappa had something different in his mind. He decided not to take me far to Mira Road East Thane from KEM hospital Parel Mumbai and keep me at Mahim Mumbai. Incase my health condition becomes serious, immediately I could be brought to K.E.M. hospital. This option was good. The toilet system was common and was outside and this was the main question. Pappa Mummy thanked everybody in the ward and we left. I was taken to Bandra East Mumbai suburban. My uncle Ravindra Anna had arranged a room in Govt. Guest House in Government Colony opposite New English High School and between 9 and 10 number buildings. K.E.M. hospital was nearby Bandra compared to Mira Road. So pappa felt OK with this option because toilet was inside the room and it was easy for me also. He thought at least I will be comfortable and I was brought there by NCP's ambulance. I was very much kept comfortable there. But my condition was more serious. All three of them mummy, pappa and Samiksha didi had kept watch on me day and night. My mummy had shouted Ravindra uncle in the KEM hospital, same issues and problems were now created in between my life saving situation at Bandra East Mumbai. By all the finance of my pappa, the rooms there which were built at Bandra East Kherwadi near Govt. Colony by my paternal grandmother Aaee, uncle Ravindra anna and my pappa in the slum. Now legal and permanent rooms of SRA were about to get in the building in the place of those slum rooooms. But purposely controversies were created on the claims and holds those personal owenerships of rooms of the family property there. 3 of my uncles and their families, aunty (Mai aatya) and Aaee (Grandmother) had word fights many a times.

Pappa did not take part in those controvercies but Pappa was finding difficulty in keeping complete watch on my condition and health there. Mummy pappa decided to check out as soon as possible from there. They were alert. My food, my medicines, my walking, my toilet, urine etc. one and many difficulties we were facing there. Pappa sent mummy and Samiksha didi on 1 14th August 2011 to Mira Road home to clean it up and fill water there and he himself stayed with me. That time my Karate Coach Mr. Pravin Shukla Sir and his sister-in-law Khushboo had come to see me there. Same day I heard Bollywood actor "Shammi Kapoor's death news on FM Radio. I had only one source of entertainment and it was mobile FM radio and I told the news to my mummy pappa and Samiksha didi. I like songs and in that critical condition also I was listening them. I told uncle Ravindra anna to bring T.V. set in my room several times. But he only promised. My childhood friend Mahendra Sakpal (Mayaa) came to see me there. His family told about me and so he came there. He straight away, without taking permission came towards me. Seeing this, suddenly my mummy stopped him. She asked, "Who are you and what do you want?" "I am Mayaa" 2-3 times he specified and then mummy remembered and recognized him. His twin brother Sanjay sakpal also had come to see me at K.E.M. hospital. Pappa, Mummy and Samiksha didi told me many such incidents later. The family matter were extreme now, Mummy and Samiksha didi cleaned our Mira Road house and came back. Next morning on 15 August 2011, mummy, pappa and Samiksha didi brought me in our home at Mira Road by taxi. "Our home is ours at the end". After coming home, I was able to see little bit I felt. I was trying hard to pronounce words but was not able to. Still I was asking several questions, "Why are we at Niwate Sir's house?" Why I am brought here?" Now also urine bag was attached to me. Vomiting was also going on. My vision was still to come. My memory was also to come. I had no balance; I had lost control on my body. I was paralysed. I was fully bed ridden. I was unsafe. I was restless. In this condition also I was trying to walk, taking my pappa's, mummy's and Dilip mama's support. Else I was made to walk by them. It was because Dr. Amit Mahore sir had told them to make me walk whole day. He told to give me "Boiled eggs and salt, Curd and salt" daily 4 times. He had said, "If salt (electrolytes) reduces in the body then he will fall unconscious! Morning, afternoon, evening followed all these things made me walk!" Pappa used the guidance of Dr. Amit Mahore sir and made me walk a lot. Didi had shooted a video of my walking and kept to show Dr. Amit Mahore sir. I was walking in legs stretched position. The distance between my legs was more. So, when we went to K.E.M. hospital for follow-up by taxi, looking at my walking Dr. Amit Mahore sir said, "Walk straight in one line." So I started trying to walk in that way. But it was not at all possible for me. Days went. 24hours mummy was with me. Before my surgery operation, my mummy would go to meet her sick mother at Dilip mama's house beside our building. But now it was stopped. Sick Mahim Aaee (mummy's mother's) health became serious. Now she was taken to Mahim. But she expired at Dnyandev mama's house in her own house at Mahim. This mountain of sorrow fell on my family and especially on my mummy. She broke down emotionally. We really felt sad. I can't even imagine what mummy's state of mind would have been. That day, Samiksha didi went to Mahim from K.C. college Curchgate Mumbai in the afternoon, last time saw our beloved maternal grandmother Mahim Aaee's face, touched her feet and came back to Mira Road. When Samiksha didi came home, to be with me, pappa took mummy to Mahim. Mummy had my responsibility and it was necessary for her to carry it. So, keeping the sorrow of her mother's death in her mind, she returned to Mira Road same evening with pappa after her own beloved mother's funeral. She had returned only for my sake! I could remember those incidents slightly. My memory was improved a bit that time and my vision was also improved a bit. Mummy's sorrow was huge. She had not been able to do anything for her parents. We also couldn't do anything more for them. Whatever caring, mercing she was able to do, she did. She would always have this feeling of regret. But keeping all the things aside, she did everything as usual for me. Being on the bed,many times I saw tears in her eyes. I could imagine and feel the state of her mind from her voice also. Taking my urine in the pot, taking me in the bathroom toilet. All those things she only was doing there with my pappa. After the death of grandmother; Mahim Aaee (mummy's mother); after 13 days rites and rituals were completed and for that also mummy went with pappa for some time and returned home soon only for me. It's true that no one can know how deep one woman's mind would be. There were two resposibilites in front of mummy in this period. Pappa and Samiksha didi only gave her emotional and mental support. But my health was improving day by day now and this was the only nice thing happening for my mummy. In these days I was not walking. So hydrocephalus (water) got collected in my back head where operation was done. There is a permanent patch where the water got collected and a swollen balloon kind of spot occurred outside of my back head. We didn't know about this and we again decided to meet Dr. Amit Mahore sir at K.E.M. hospital. We went by taxi to Parel, Mumbai. We reached there. Dr. Amit Mahore sir checked me and said "It's all fine, keep the routine continued". Looking at my back head he said, "His shunt VP tube is not working properly. (Tube which is gone from brain to urinary bladder from my body). Dr. Amit Mahore sir said, "We will see ahead what we can do?" But we got afraid again.

He also said, "How many times we will operate him?" We were told to go home for this time. We came down in tensed and sat in the KEM's hospital canteen itself. Pappa went out to bring me juice. I was strong with the mind. I wished in my mind that let a solution be there on this problem. Same time Dr. Amit Mahore sir gave a call. "Where are you all now?" Dr. Amit Mahore sir asked. Mummy replied, "We are here only, in the KEM's canteen." He said, "Come quickly to 10 No. ward with Suhas!" We were again in tension!. Immediately pappa came there. We told him about the doctor's call. He said, "First eat something, drink juice and water; then we'll go in the ward." Any how I had mosambi (sweet lime) juice in 5 minutes. Mummy, pappa Samiksha didi took tea and we then reached 10 No. Ward once again. Dr. Amit Mahore sir said, "Good that you came back. We'll remove his water (hydrocephalus) here now." How will the water (hydrocephalus) be removed? We didn't know. He said, "We will tie a turban round your head. You have to wear it!" I became happy hearing it. I was made to sit on the cot-bed. I sat fearlessly with pappa's support. Whole team of Dr. Amit Mahore sir stood around my bed. He said, "The water will be removed by an injection". I, my mummy, my pappa and my Samiksha didi went blank for a moment. Mummy stayed far away from my bed. Both my hands were caught tightly. One of the team mate doctor applied surgical spirit on my back head. Immediately other doctor injected a long needle in my swollen spot back head. There was no end of pain and I couldn't express it. Behind the needle, they attached an injection vacuum gun. Keeping the needle inside they sucked water by the vacuum gun 4 times. I was statue; because Dr. Amit Mahore sir told me not to do any movement. They did this keeping in mind that the needle must stay away from my brain. It shouldn't touch my brain. And after the removal of the needle, my back head was not only flat but also got compressed and the swollen balloon went inside. Now there was no extra accumulated water (hydrocephalus) in my head. For time being this solution had worked and was effective. A tight pink cotton woolen bandage, turban like (Sunny Deol wears in Jeet Movie) was tightly tied around my head from back side of my head and especially my back head spot from where water (hydrocephalus) was removed. Now we were told to go home. Pappa arranged a taxi and we four came straight to Mira Road. While travelling many times I went to urine. I didn't had have "fit" issue. Still "Eptoine" tablet was given to me because brain surgery was done. I was recovering slowly and steadily. Pappa, mummy and Samiksha didi had to manage everything. The urine bag was attached to my bed at home. Pappa attached a condom catcher to me and I would sleep. I would take 250gms. Of curd and with 4 T-spoon of salt in it and drink it. And followed by medicines. Same in the afternoon and in the evening also and boiled egg was a day with salt; and I would eat lunch and dinner. Then I started having breakfast, lunch in which 4 bhakries, vegetables, rice and dal. Same was repeated in my dinner. I was not having any spicy, heat generated things. Still boils started to come on my skin and body. Firstly they were small, then they became big. New blood started coming from them. Pappa told Dr. Amit Mahore sir about this on phone. Again there was a new problem. But he asked, "Which medicines are going on?" Pappa told, "Eptoin Tablet, that to twice a day!" Dr.Amit Mahore sir replied, "Stop it!". The boils were cracking and blood was falling on the floor. Looking this, Samiksha didi cried a lot. By the suggestion of Dr. Amit Mahore sir, pappa took me to the Skin expert, dermatologist in Mira Road. He was Dr. Pramod Bhandari sir. He has clinic in Sheetal Nagar, near MTNL,

Mira Road. Pappa went there and took an appointment. By autorickshaw, mummy, pappa took me there with my file. Everybody in the clinic was looking at me. Once or twice I had gone to urine. I did it in the pot and pappa went out and washed the pot then. My number came. Mummy, pappa took me inside the cabin. I was able to see bit clear now. Looking at me, my file and hearing my case history from pappa, Dr. Pramod Bhandari sir was shocked. He checked me. He saw my boils by magnifying glass and gave tablets, cream and soap and told us to visit again in 10 days. Soon I had a positive effect of his treatment. Slowly we started understanding what to eat what to avoid. Which food is allergic, many things were understood bygetting experience. As pappa informed in writing; TATA Hospital Parel, Mumbai got news of my third brain surgery. There was TATA Hospital's follow up again. We four had gone there. Dr. Rakesh Jalali sir was sitting in front. Many times I had asked mummy, pappa and Samiklsha didi why my health became worst before 3rd surgery. I had eaten corn and so had the loose motions a lot, then my condition became serious, pappa told me once. Exactly same thing, I told Dr. Rakesh Jalali sir of TATA Hospital Parel, Mumbai and he started smiling and said, "Tumour doesn't increase because of corn!" It was my and pappa's misunderstanding; now I understood. Dr. Rakesh Jalali sir suggested to do "Shunt VP replacement surgery. "It takes 10 minutes for this surgery; Do I tell Dr. Dattatray Mujumdar?" Dr. Rakesh Jalali asked pappa. But papa immediately said, "We will think and then let you know". Pappa had told us an important thing. Telling things of K.E.M. hospital doctors to TATA hospital doctors is making them fight. Keeping this thing in mind, pappa avoided the telling of suggestions of one doctor to other. Dr. Amit Mahore sir had strictly warned us to follow and trust only one doctor. Pappa followed this rule and we decided to go ahead with the guidance of Dr. Amit Mahore sir of K.E.M. Hospital. He had taken out hydrocephalus by injection from my back head spot and turban was tied to my head. Thereafter my shunt VP tube started working. First shunt VP tube was only 50% working but when the hydrocephallus (water) was removed from back head swollen spot; shunt VP tube started working 75%. We did one M.R.I. Scan and showed to Dr. Amit Mahore sir as per his suggestion. He said, "Now the shunt VP tube is working nicely; more than 75% it started to work". And so my 4th brain surgery was avoided. We all were happy. Our relatives were trying to come to see me. But because of pappa's suggestion, they were avoiding. He said, "At one time where actually can we pay attention? "Look after the guests or to look after my care?" Pappa took a big decision in this critical situation. But then also fro, Panvel;m Khandeshwar Mahendra kaka, Kalpana Kaki, Sonu baba, Saro Aaee, Vikesh (dadu), Arti Vahini, Bipin (Bhau), Rakesh from Ghatkopar, Sunil Tatya and Sarika Kaki came to see me. Pappa told Milind bhaee uncle to do the arrangements of their food, breakfast at his house in beside building at his place. Many relatives then also came and they fell shocked seeing my critical condition. Pappa Mummy and didi had 24 hours watch on my health. Many times I vomited because of over eating. But as of the guidance of Dr. Amit Mahore sir, I kept eating and drinking no matter; I vomited or had loose motions. Many times in a day all three made me walk and practice it. I also would respond to them and walk. Sometimes I would feel lazy to walk. My eye sight had improved now and was able to see a bit. My pappa's dear friend Mr. Prakash Pandurang Niwate Sir gave a VCD of a movie to watch. I didn't ask him about what the VCD. is; but he insisted me to watch it and listen to it properly. I started watching T.V., but sitting closely. It was a joke or fun because I felt hungry in the midnight too. So mummy would keep some food for me to eat. I would desire to have variety of fast food to eat. But pappa told me to avoid them strictly. I would listen to him as well. Some time he would also feel pitty on me. Just take it he would say. I started having banana chips. In the midnight mummy kept food for me but if I would feel more hungry then I had chips, nuts, a jaggery brittle (chikki). I avoided chocolates. Some things were easy to digest and some I found hard to digest. So I ate those things which I found easy to digest. Dr. Amit Mahore sir had said, "Feed him, hydrate him and make him walk!". We kept in mind his words and strictly followed them and learned from our own mistakes and experiences. I couldn't speak words, pronounce them clearly. Main organs and whole body was affected by the brain surgery. I had lost control on my body. But because of self-determination, self-power, self-desire to come out of this situation and strictly following doctor's instructions helped me to overcome the hurdles. This, I was able to do because of Karate practice, for more than 12 years. I had great power of pain bearing, a good resistance power, but sometime I would collapse from my mind. I got scared. But looking at the fight of my mummy pappa and Samiksha didi for saving my life. Looking at their faces I again get stable. If a fallen person doesn't desire to stand up again, doesn't wish to get up again, if he is not willing to stand; then none can make and help him stand again. If we have will power; if we wish; if we have desire; then only we can overcome all the hurdles, all the problems! I have learnt this. Many funny incidents occurred with me. I thought to speak one word and other word would come out from me. Once I was having food and finished it and I wanted tablet to eat so just made a move on the cot; I lost my balance; I fell on the cot bed; but one thing I did;, I was catching a glass of water tightly in my hand and I didn't let it fall on bed. Not a single drop also. When mummy pappa and Samiksha didi brought me in our complex (colony) to walk, everybody would see what efforts they were taking to make me get well soon. Boys playing cricket would stop for some time when I was made to walk. Only once they were told to stop then they would start playing after I had returned home. I would walk like a crab having distance in both legs. Dr. Amit Mahore sir told me practice walking in one straight line. I prasticed it with efforts and I had a normal walking now. In further follow-ups in TATA hospital, Dr. Savita Goswami madam and Dr. Lekhika madam would take my various I.Q. (intelligent quotient) tests.

Dr. Ajay Dudhani sir, eye expert at Santacruz West Mumbai; referred by TATA Hospital would do my eye sight treatment. He had some machineries which very few big hospitals had in Mumbai. There is a eye sight checking machine where we have to hit points by trigger. One of my eyeball would be closed by cotton ball and tape was put on it. Then in machine, there is a red light small point in the center. Looking at that point without moving eyeball right or left if a green light blinking would be seen them I pressed the trigger. The machine would note it. Same procedure would be repeated for other eye ball. I had to keep my chin on the stand ending inside the machine which is box rectangle type. While the test is on, all the lights are off in that room. Miss Bharti Sawant, who is nurse there would take print of the test. While reaching the brain tumour, the blood vessels of eyes were cut. So my right eye ball is loose and so it shifts/ squints and my vision gets tilted/squinted, squinted with overlapped image. For this the test is done and is necessary. Dr. Ajay Dudhani sir has told me to do a computerized laser eye surgery for it also. But how much risk to take and how many surgeries to undergo? And money to spend? So pappa said, we will see what to do ahead!" I always had a depressed mindset. All my friends completed their studies, doing jobs, going out, meeting each other and I was left alone. Understanding my situation, my elder sister Samiksha didi would call all my friends on my birthday 6th May and when they would come, I was fully charged up. Dr. Prashant Ghorpade, Chef Nikhil Kamble, Prathamesh Gharat, Adv. Shiraj Manjrekar, Rupesh Bhosle, Durgadas Rathod, Amit Wani all would come. My school teacher Mrs. Greta Pharel had come to see me. My other teachers also came to see me. Mrs. Renuka Harmalkar, Mrs. Usha Shridhar, Mrs. Sible Furtado, Mrs. Loretta Pinto and Mrs. Sarita Vaz, Mrs.Enid Lemos teacher; Greta Pharel teacher had brought them. I touched everyone's feet and took their blessings. We sang songs together also. Mrs. Vasudha Ghag is aged so mummy pappa and I went to her place. My Karate Sir, Mr. Pravin Shukla, my guru comes to see me from starting when I got ill till today. All the teachers and my gurus have an attachment with me. They love me and care for me. I feel blessed and lucky. Everyone from start has cared, prayed and did efforts for my good health. I am thankful to all and will be for life time. This is my second birth. Many incidents I remember and some I have forgotten. Those which I memorized, I have written, rest if possible I will write in future. K.E.M. hospital's doctors from Parel Mumbai and my surgeon Dr. Amit Mahore sir had told us to call him any time; if we have any doubt and problem regarding my health. Accordingly we would call him and take his guidance. TATA hospital's Dr. Rakesh Jalali sir (radiation and oncology expert) has founded B.T.F. (Brain Tumour Foundation). Because of this many patients who cannot afford the fees of treatment; they are free of charges for radiation. My brain surgeries were done in K.E.M. hospital and its B.M.C. undertaking Govt. Medical College and Hospital (Bombay Municipal Hospital). It is connected to TATA hospital because poor patients, common man can't afford big hospitals and the radiation fees. So after surgery they are sent to TATA hospital. There are hospitals of Municipal Corporations; State Government and Central Government which are affiliated to TATA Hospital Parel, Mumbai. B.T.F. is independent and every year it arranges Art Mela, Singing and Dancing programmes where the patients perform. The patients who are healed and healing also come and take part in it. Their relatives also join. Till today I have sung many songs which inspires and motivates my patients friends and their relatives. They get encouragement by it. "Lehro Se Darr Kar Nauka Paar Nahi Hoti, Koshish Karne walon ki kabhi haar nahi hoti" (Afraiding the Tides won't reach ship to the sea shore and people who keep trying never get defeated). This poem of poet" Harivanshrai Bacchan" which is an inspiring and motivational poem; I had performed there many times. Pappa had made me practice the poem and showed how to perform and when I performed it; everyone liked it. This was in 2013. In the year 2010, I met famous music director and singer ; Salim Merchant at B.T.F. Annual Function. I got a chance to sing a song in front of him. I took opportunity and sang 2 songs there. Like this many famous people are called by Dr. Rakesh Jalali sir; in the annual function of B.T.F. Everyone is encouraged and made happy by this. In the same program next year; the music director Jatin Pandit also came with his family there. They performed and entertained everyone. ISNO (Indian Society of Neuro Oncology) and ASNO (Asian Society of Neuro Oncology) had annual meeting in Mumbai at Hotel Taj for 5 days. On the last day, all patients and their relatives were called there. Many great doctors from all over the World had taken part. The formula of tablet Neurobian Forte who invented that World level Dr. Dennis Strongman had also come to meet all of us. All the doctors from the Summit were praising the work of Dr. Rakesh Jalali sir. I had less interest in the Art Mela there. I was mesmerized looking at the interior, marble work, designing, lamps, eating and drinking variety facilities in Taj Hotel. Not only me everyone was mesmerized there. But I sang a very nice song there; As expected, pappa had taken practice of my singing. The song was "Ehsaan mere dil pe tumhara hai doston". Everybody were around me clapping and enjoying the song. I sang OK, fine and all appreciated it too. From years; Dr. Rakesh Jalali sir, TATA hospital and his team; Miss Naina Godamble mam , Jayashree mam , Sneha mam, Dr. Shashikant Chandanshive (before), Dr. Mansi Takle (my time); etc. people try to make the patient and their family feel special and fill happiness in their lives. In the year 2014, T.V. Serial actor, actress "Bhide Sir and Daya mam from SAB TV serial Taarak Mehta Ka Ulta Chasma had come. I met Disha mam (Dayaben). She also spoke with my mummy. A person was from the country of Slovakia; his name was Brano Pollock; Dr. Rakesh Jalali sir specially introduced me to Mr. Brano Pollock and told about me. I am in contact with him through e-mail via internet. My dear friend Ashish Kanekar from "Khed Maharashtra; was a former patient like me; is also in contact with me. Many patients are there; whose condition has drastically changed now I feel happy when I meet them. What were they and now what a positive change I see in them. Some do job, some are in business field. This is indeed a second birth to every one there. I am also a member of "Ugam foundation". But I am not able to attend it. Dr. Savita Goswami; my TATA Hospital 's psychologist expert is one of head of Ugam Foundation. Once pappa and I had gone in it on call from her. Its in Parel Mumbai and lots of travelling is there. Because of my balance problem and vision problem I avoided it. Taking note about my successful fight against Brain Tumour Cancer; V-Care Foundation also felicitated and honoured me with a trophy by hands of famous celebrity and Hindi Bollywood Movie actress in song "Sapne me militia hai "fame Shefali Shah. I performed a poem's four lines on that occasion. One and many like this. I am getting experiences now. Whole life of mine has changed. Not only I was saved from the deadly brain cancer disease but also I was kept alive and secured by my doctors and my relatives. My school friends Chetan Naik and Sneha Kudtarkar came to see me at my place. Then on one of my birthday ;Sneha Kudtarkar brought cake for me with my other friends. My school friend Santoshi Kadam had visited our house to meet me. Rishabh Desai and Pranit Dhopte also came to see my health.

When I was unable to get up on my own and was unable to give voice in the night then I made a pinching sound with my thumb and middle finger (chutaki). Hearing this sound one of the three from my mummy, pappa and Samiksha didi immediately got up and took care of me.

In this critical condition of mine in 2012 my elder sister Samiksha didi got married with Prof. Ravindra Prakash Suryavanshi; Vadmurabi; Devani ;Latur;Maharashtra. Looking at my improvement in health; my Pappa decided to let her marry. Because of this wedding function there was a new pleasure and happiness in our lives. In 2015; I became Mama (uncle) playing with Little Master Aharta (Bala) my nephew (sister's son).

I became more and more happy and got well. I also got married in 2017. But my wife left me with merciless cruelty in 2018. I was broken physically and emotionally alone in sorrow. But still I am living courageously with my mummy and pappa. My mummy-pappa are my real wealth in my bad financial crises. I now the man of brain damage trying coaching; teaching; working for the brain development; brain gyming of the children through Japaneese Sorban Abacus Mathematics by Versatile Educare System (VES) Mumbai; by Prof.Ajay Darekar sir. I don't have financial stability but I am trying to give knowledge to the children with the help of my remaining brain power by this noble teaching profession. With the help of my rebirth's hands and remaining brain power; I am trying to develop brains of all my students; making them progressive, positive and prosperative. I have humbly left everything else in the hands of universal five elements, powers and control management system and have left my future, destiny in their hands.

Welfare luck to all.

This was the story of my rebirth; is; and to be continued....

----Suhas.....

=====

My Dear & Respected Teachers Of Cardinal Gracious High School Bandra (E), Mumbai, Who Tried Their Best To Support Me.

FORM LEFT / MY DEAR AND RESPECTED TEACHERMRS. SIBLE FURTADO, MRS. GRETA PHARIL, MRS. SARITA VAZ, MRS. LORETTA PINTO, MRS. ENID LEMOSOF CARDINAL GRACIOUS HIGH SCHOOL BANDRA (E), MUMBAI AT OUR HOUSE 2013 AFTER MY RECOVERY

I AM WITH MY DEAR AND RESPECTED TEACHER MRS. VASUDHA GHAGH OF CARDINAL AFTER MY RECOVERY 2013 I VISITED HER HOUSE WITH MY PERENTS

FROM LEFT/ MY DEAR AND RESPECTED TEACHERS MRS. RENUKA HARMALKAR ANDMRS. USHA SHRIDHAR OF CARDINAL AFTER MY RECOVERY 2013.

I AM WITH MY DEAR & RESPECTED PROF. MRS. RUCHA R. SOMAN AND MRS.ARCHANA V. MATE MADAM OF MAHATMA PHULE TECHNICAL HIGH SCHOOL & JUNIOR COLLEGE, BHOIWADA PAREL MUMBAI, AFTER MY RECOVERY 2016.

My Dear & Respected Friends Who Tried Their Best To Support Me

FROM LEFT PRATHAMESH GHARAT, DURGADAS RATHOD, NIKHIL KAMBLE,
SHIRAJ MAJREKAR, RUPESH BHOSLE, PRASHANT GHORPADE, SITTING - AMIT WANIIN OUR HOUSE AFTER MY RECOVERY ON MY BIRTHDAY IN 2009.

I AM WITH MANGESH CHOUDHARY (MIDDLE) ABHISHEKH MORE, IN MY HOUSE AFTER MY RECOVERY IN 2014

After My Three Surgeries & Recoveries I Involved In Btf's Motivational Programs Held In Tata Memorial Hospital, Parel Mumbai & Taj Hotel Mumbai

I A I AM WITH SLOVAKIAN DONAR OF BTFMR. BRANO POLLOCK AT TATA MEMORIAL HOSPITAL PAREL MUMBAI,AT ART MELA & ANNUAL FUNCTION OF BTF AFTER MY RECOVERY 2013. WITH SLOVAKIAN DONAR OF BTFMR. BRANO POLLOCK AT TATA MEMORIAL HOSPITAL PAREL MUMBAI,AT ART MELA & ANNUAL FUNCTION OF BTF AFTER MY RECOVERY 2013.

I AM WITH FAMOUS BOLLYWOOD MUSICIAN MR.SALIM MERCHANT AT TATA MEMORIAL HOSPITAL PAREL MUMBAI,AT ART MELA & ANNUAL FUNCTION OF BTF 2010.

I AM WITH FAMOUS TV SERIAL'S ACTRESS (DAYABEN'S CHARECTER OF TARAK MEHTA KA ULTA CHASMA) DISHA VAKANI MADAM AT TATA MEMORIAL HOSPITAL PARELMUMBAI IN ART MELA 2014.

My Three Brain Tumour Cancer Surgeries In Kem Hospital Parel Mumbai And My Rebirth's Critical Conditions And Situations.

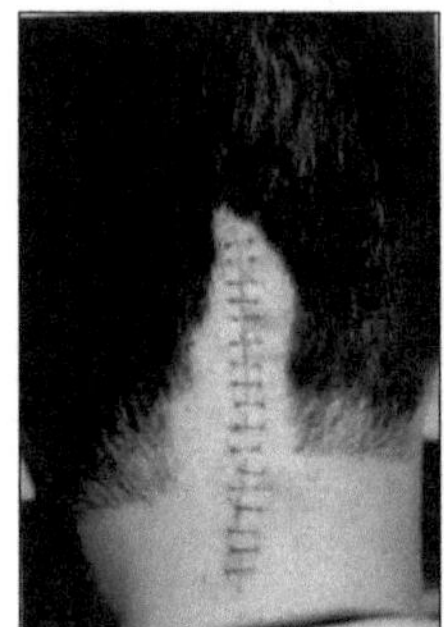

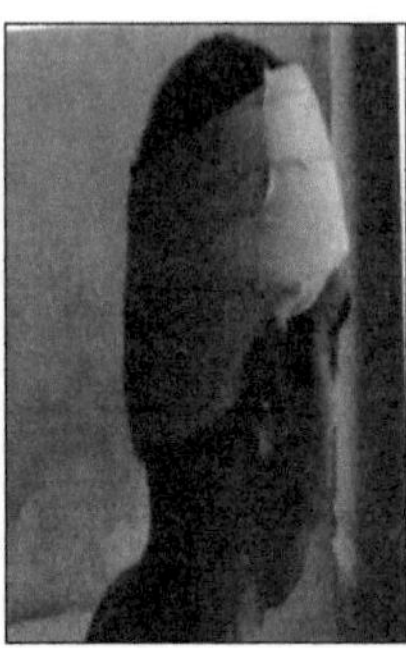

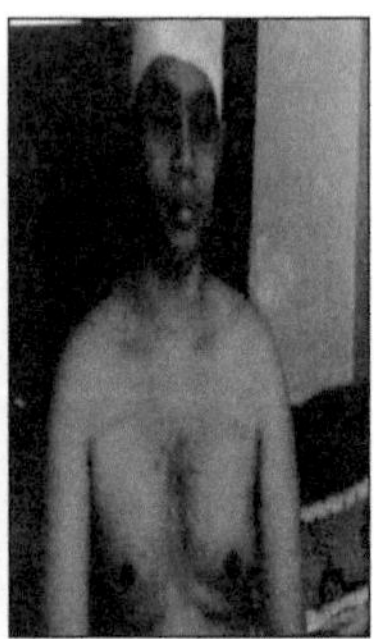

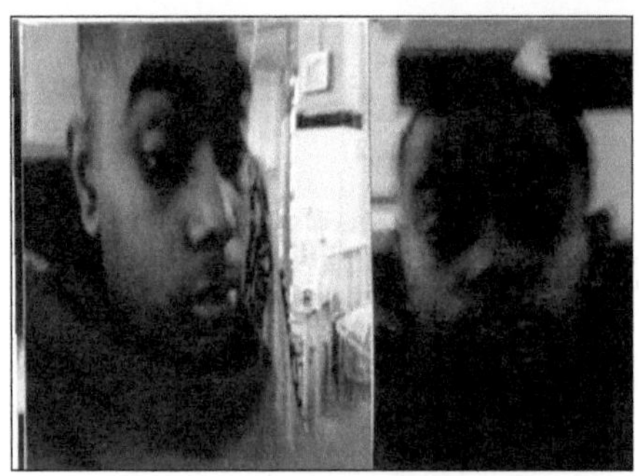

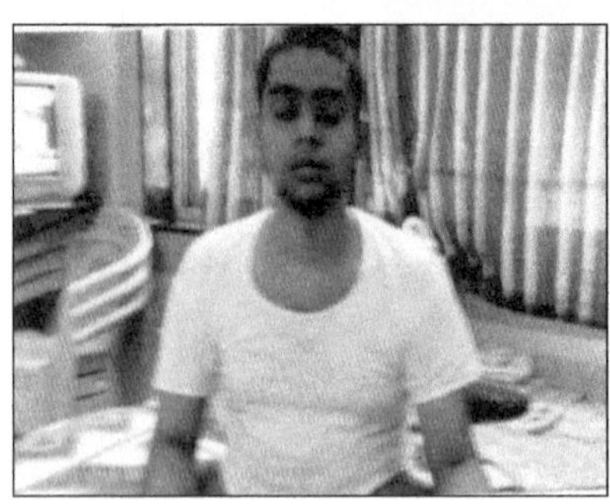

After last surgery with the pandage at the back head 2nd floor in ward no 10 at KEM Hospital Parel Mumbai

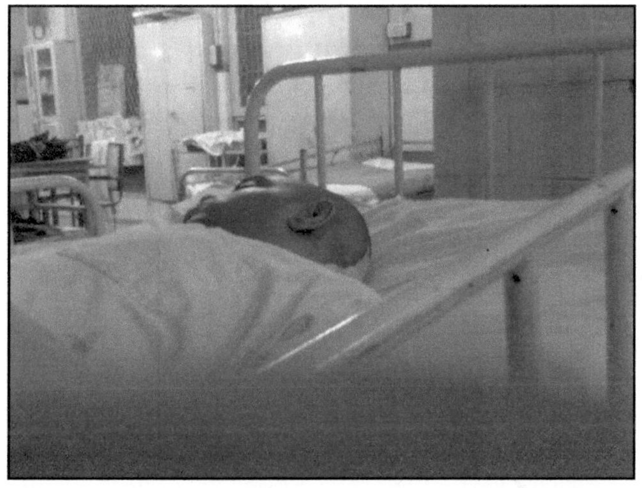

The Story Of MyRebirth

English Autobiography

Author - Bhaoo / Suhas

Mr. Suhas Surendra Sumita Jadhav Bsc (Ii Year)

Dob - 6-5-1989 /Mahim / Mumbai

Kudli : Guhagar ; Ratnagiri Maharashtra ; India

Ravi Chintan : 3/204; Gaurav Sankalpa ; Ravi Group;Phase-1 ; Near Shanti Vidya Nagari ; Mira Road(East); District - Thane :-401107.

Education : Cardinal Gracious High School ;Kherwadi ; Bandra (East); Mumbai-400051; Upto Ss.C, English Medium

Mahatma Phule Technical High School

Junior College, Bhoiwada; Parel; Mumbai - 400012

Vidyavardhini's Vartak College Of Science ; Vasai (West); 401202

* ***Hobbies***

Singing; Reading; Listening Music, Oratory

* ***Favorite Subjects :***

English; Marathi; Hindi; History; Economics

* **Special Interests :** Spirituality And Philosophy

* **Work Space :** Japaneese Soroban Abacus Mathematics(Ves);Guide Prof. Ajay Darekar Sir

* ***Achievements:***

Head Boy Of Cardinal Gracious High School Kherwadi Bandra (East);Mumbai-51; In 2004-2005

Shotokan Karate Trainning

Black Belt Ist Dan Refery Licence Holder

* **Karate Coach** Mr. K.N.S. Pillai Sir Mr. Pravin Shukla Sir

9 789356 114388

Printed by Libri Plureos GmbH in Hamburg,
Germany